The Shining Brother

The Shining Brother

Laurence Temple

Gateway Books, London

First edition 1941
Second edition 1970
This third edition published 1984
by GATEWAY BOOKS
37 Upper Addison Gardens
London W14 8AJ
in collaboration with
THE COLLEGE OF PSYCHIC STUDIES
16 Queensberry Place
London SW7

British Library Cataloguing in Publication Data

Temple, Laurence
    The Shining Brother.
    1. Spirit writings
    I. Title
    133.9'3   BF1301
    ISBN 0-946551-06-5

Printed and bound in Great Britain
by Photobooks (Bristol) Ltd

TO

SANTA CHIARA

Not the voice, but the vow;
Not clamour, but love,
Not the stringed instrument, but the heart,
Sounds in the ear of God.

From the choir of Saint Damian, Assisi

FOREWORD TO THIRD EDITION

IT is indeed good that this beautiful little book should be republished, for it is timeless and eternal. It offers the story of a direct and living contact between St Francis and one who was Brother Leo, his leading follower in the days at Assisi. Assuredly, for a mind that is unprejudiced and open, the truth of this claim is convincing.

In our generation we stand upon a threshold at which the barrier to the supersensible worlds is thinning and indeed crumbling. It is an age in which holistic thinking emerges as a vital factor in facing a period of crisis and change. We recover the vision that the human being is spirit, soul and body, and that the kernel of a man or woman, that which can say "I", is a droplet of Divinity and therefore imperishable and immortal. As a spark of God it always was and always will be. What a prospect!

Thus the great soul which was Francis, that wonderful bearer of the Christ Impulse of compassion for all life, is alive for evermore, and of course must be in action in the age of the Second Coming, when the Christ Love and Power floods again into humanity for its redemption. Nothing is more probable than that the onetime "little poor man of Assisi" should rally his followers and re-enter the stream of earth consciousness.

In our death-ridden culture the most vital thing is the reassessing (dare we say the "debunking") of death. Indeed we see that death is really the great educator, to awaken us to the truth that for this human core there can be no dying. It is alive, and Life is indestructible.

This is a book that carries conviction. Laurence Temple, as Brother Laurence, or "Leo" of the Franciscan story, found that he could fully accept that the spirit of his Master Francis really had come back with his message for our time. The book contains a number of direct communications from St. Francis, written in the 1930s when the storm warnings of war were rising. They read today with immediate force for our own situation, and they can fill us with courage. Listen to this sentence:

" This is a day of days when many forces meet and much is shattered in the impact; yet in the Infinite Mind is the Supreme Thought, the Creative Urge towards perfection, and we who dwell in the Eternal Harmony are at one with those vast waves of power, and all our being is given to the invincible direction of the thought forms of God."

We may see that behind calamity and cataclysm is the Power of God, cleansing and transforming the planet.

" For the soul of man requireth freedom for the growth of the new age and strength to carry the burden of greater responsibilities. Therefore upon many will be poured forth the Gifts of the Spirit, that light may penetrate the darkness and humanity be reborn nearer to the Divine Image."

Here is the factor wholly ignored in our political and economic efforts to solve the vast planetary problems we have caused. Here are the forgotten allies without whom we cannot solve those problems. Through this power the planet can be cleansed and a new age ushered in. For God is on the march!

That Francis, that Christed figure, should communicate is wonderful and lovely. *The Shining Brother* is another most positive contribution to the thinning of the veil. Reading it brings joy and love. And, truly, what is happening to us now is that Love, as an energy released, is pouring through the material world as a transforming force.

The Earth is to be cleansed. Glory be! This is the age of the Second Coming. One soul after another is waking up to this stupendous truth. The Christ Power comes alive in the human heart, truly His temple. And then we know that the same Divinity is in every other heart and shines from other eyes. So the Love may sweep through the human layer, the no sphere. This will seem like Apocalyptic thinking, of course, to those still adhering to the old paradigm of greed, egoism, violence and aggression, like the riding of the Four Horsemen. But since the world is outwardly so mad and so bad, it is totally valid to throw our thinking into this supreme hope of transformation in our time. To quote lines from a sonnet by Sidney Royse Lysaght:

" . . . We have seen loveliness that shall not pass
    We have beheld immortal destinies
    We have known Heaven and Hell and joined their
    strife
Aye we, whose flesh shall perish as the grass
    Have flung the passion of the heart that dies
    Into the hope of everlasting life."

Read this story and let its living joy flow through your veins and enlighten heart and mind.

GEORGE TREVELYAN, BT

January, 1984.

INTRODUCTION TO FIRST EDITION

THIS book contains a narrative of events relating to the inward and outward progress of an active professional man who describes how strangely he was brought to know unseen guidance and how he gained more alert awareness of the invisible world.

Some will look for evidence that the narrative is not based on imagination; others, being already convinced of the reality of communication with the discarnate, will wish to learn what these can tell of their present life and surroundings. Something of both will be found in this book, but it stresses a further and outstanding feature.

I was present at a gathering of clergy where speakers had described the evidence on which they based assurance that relatives beyond death had spoken to them through psychic channels. In subsequent discussion someone remarked that, instead of messages from uncles and parents, he would prefer to hear what some great saint of olden days could tell about life in Heaven and the reason for man's being on earth. Readers who share that preference will find unusual interest in the sayings of Francis here recorded.

And who is this Francis, whose sayings fill so considerable a portion of the book? Is he, indeed, the world-famous founder of the Franciscan Order who left this world centuries ago?

Compelling evidence of identity is more easily established by relatives, because they and we have memories in common to which allusion can be made and which are private to ourselves. Those who lived further back would find it difficult to offer any evidence for their identity which was not common knowledge or, at least, knowledge easily accessible to the public. Therefore, in order to satisfy critical minds, such communicators would need to offer a different type of evidence: such as we find in these messages from Francis. It consists in appeal to the deeper feelings, the finer intuitions, and in the manifestation of characteristics which were strongly marked in the life of the communicator. The characteristics of Saint Francis appear in these recorded messages.

Such evidence will vary in its compulsion according to the reader's receptivity. The author records with care and frankness the effect they made on his inmost thought and feeling, and his progressive reaction to them.

Clearly then, in order to estimate the value of this story, it is necessary to know something of the narrator. And it is here that I may perhaps testify from personal acquaintance with him. He is a man of advancing middle age, a Fellow of the Royal Institute of British Architects, and still active in his profession. During the period through which this story runs, he was usually engrossed with such mundane matters as calculations, prices, measurements, the quality of building material, and discussions with building committees. This is scarcely the atmosphere in which fantastic imaginings and poetic dreamings flourish. In conversation, he is quite the reverse of that. One would not hesitate to take his word on any matter of fact, confident that he was a quick and exact thinker, an acute observer, and of strictly logical mind.

He has set down for us with careful precision the order of events as these came to his notice. He shows us the variety of facts on which his conclusions are based and how gradually conviction took form.

Readers will learn that, on January 30th, 1932, it was foretold that, in the coming years, he would build many churches, and that this was to be a prominent feature of his work. At that time there was nothing to suggest any such future for his professional career. I have been permitted to inspect the list of ecclesiastical buildings which he designed in the subsequent years. He had previously done some decorative work for these churches and had built one church which is well known to me. This is alluded to in the book as Hilborough Church. It was completed in 1930.

Counting from 1932, I find that the author has designed seventeen places of worship and also carried out fifteen commissions for alteration or addition to existing churches. At present he is discussing plans for eighteen more churches and for seven church halls or schoolrooms, with their respective building committees.

This list represents a striking change in the nature of work which, previously, had been concerned with residential and business premises. We, who now view the forecast in the light of its fulfilment, can appreciate its significance. It reveals a plan and purpose which were unknown to the author. What is one to say of this?

Many have been aware of the intuitive flash which reveals suddenly a new conception of their future course; others have received with the same certainty, but gradually, a glimpse of such purpose. But, surely very few have been informed so plainly and in spoken words, of the work they were "called" to do. It requires an active imagination to share the author's feelings on realising that he could no longer escape the conviction that he was under the friendly supervision and guidance of that Saint Francis of Assisi who left earth so long ago and whose work and personality had strongly appealed to him.

The unfolding of this narrative brings before us, from an unusual angle, the perplexing question of reincarnation. Can I believe that this is not my first experience of earthly life?

That, although in another body I have lived, worked, and died, I am now returned to earth with no recollection of that past? To some minds this belief has seemed to explain the seeming injustices and inequalities with which life abounds. Whether it be fact or only fancy, the suggestion that one has been here before appeals to the romantic and, to some at least, it suggests a clue to those intuitions which in childhood and even since have puzzled those who felt them. But, if true, how is it we do not remember that previous life?

Memory should not be confused with intuition or with instinct; for memory, as we ordinarily speak of it, is a reviving of impressions received through our brain, that brain which we now possess. Such impressions are personal to one's self and may be strong or weak. The intenser impressions are easily recollected. An emotional incident impresses itself without effort on our part. It was the difficulty of being interested in certain of our school lessons which made their remembrance so uncertain.

The crucial question is this: what will happen if the deepest self within us, the soul, has received impressions with which our present brain has had no connection, impressions received when the soul was inhabiting a different body? Obviously, such impressions, not having passed through our present brain, will not "click" with it, will not be easily reproduced in consciousness as are our everyday memories.

But, although we cannot remember them, we may, perhaps at odd times and under elusive conditions, "feel" or "sense" them. If and when this happens, should they be considered as *our own*, or the dim perception of experiences which came to *another*? In other words, am I the same person as the one who, with a different body and another framework of experiences, lived before? What exactly constitutes personal identity?

It has been suggested that one's actual self is much greater than the present union of soul and body now on earth; that it may be likened, by crude analogy, to a wheel with spokes, only one of which touches earth at any one time, while the others are on their way to descend in turn for a brief contact with ground. On this analogy, the hub represents the complete soul in which are centrally united its several aspects, as spokes are united to the centre of a wheel. Experiences gained by each successive residence on earth would be added to those previously won. Thus the actual, or complete soul, would be far richer in experience than any single one of its successive earthly aspects.

On some such hypothesis it may be conceived that one is actually in relationship with past earthly lives, although practically separate and isolated as regards memory. Then, in some Grand Hereafter, these several aspects of the individual soul's experience will become united. When that is accomplished, the completely assembled soul will be in a position to survey all its previous earth-lives, as we now survey the successive experiences of childhood, adolescence, maturity, and age, thinking of them separately, while yet realising that they are all part of our own individual career.

Whatever may be our ideas about reincarnation, the narrative unfolded in this book will be found suggestive of a deeper meaning than the term is usually held to indicate.

If we have been on earth before, shall we need to return again? Will not that be decided by the progress in character we are now making? It was the boy who neglected his lessons who had to return to them for further study. Shall we be like that schoolboy? There comes to mind the saying of a former Prime Minister whom someone tried to interest in the theory that the British were the Lost Ten Tribes. He replied that he had no opinion on the question but that, as a politician, it was his business to see that we did not get lost again! That, as it seems to me, is the one practical aspect of the reincarnation hypothesis.

C. DRAYTON THOMAS

May, 1940.

THE FIRST BOOK

I

THE story I have to tell must, of necessity, be more or less autobiographical. I wish it could be written otherwise, but that appears to be impossible.

The idea in my mind is to gather together the psychic experiences of about eleven years and preface them with one or two earlier happenings.

Between the summer of 1928 and the summer of 1939 I have met by personal desire, or by chance, seventeen psychics, who have all, curiously enough, and mostly quite independently, told me the same thing. And during that time I have met none who have omitted to refer to it. The point upon which all agreed was that Saint Francis of Assisi was my personal friend and guardian.

If that association sounds fantastic to the reader, I can only assure him that on a thousand occasions I have thought exactly the same thing.

I shall tell the story precisely as it happened and in proper sequence. Except for the very earliest manifestations, I have kept careful notes. These notes consist of about one hundred and twenty thousand words or a little more than four hundred foolscap pages, annotated and dated.

By far the greater proportion of these pages consist of actual automatic scripts, of which there are one hundred and sixty-four. One hundred and thirty of these are from one source, and, as will appear later, were unsought. Several pages are reports of sittings, in which case, the accounts were written mostly within two hours of the sitting from notes taken while the medium was speaking.

Sometimes I have been given messages during ordinary conversations with people who were mediumistic. All such things will be duly indicated as the book proceeds. There have, of course, been defective sittings, surprisingly few, considering the humanity of those working on this side. Perhaps a dozen phrases have been suspect in the four volumes of notes with me now.

The perfect message, it seems to me, requires not only a dedicated medium, but a sitter also dedicated to spiritual service. When the scripts have failed, it has mostly been when one or the other has weakened in that particular respect. " If there be any self-seeking," said Thomas à Kempis, " behold this it is that hindereth thee."

II

There have been hundreds of messages. I think it would be allowable to say that during some periods I have been besieged. However cautious and sceptical one may be, obstinacy cannot live for ever under such a bombardment as I have known.

But, leaving all that, what actually is my attitude to the communications gathered together in this book ?

In the first place, I find I cannot read them without a sense stealing over me that I am in the presence of Holiness. I have to admit that, in Sabatier's phrase : " The Presence is there, under our very eyes the bush is burning."

The Little Flowers, and the two or three other Franciscan books : *The Legend of the Three Companions*, *The Mirror of Perfection*, and so forth, produce in my mind the sense of supernatural romance. It is this same effect which makes the scripts of this book impressive to me.

There have been many occasions when I would like to have considered the communications presented here as mere fantasy, due to queer and perhaps mixed mental causes ; to hidden interactions between various minds projected somehow into writing or speech.

But, although I can never fully accept all these communications, I can yet never dismiss them. I never see myself exactly filling the role indicated in the scripts. I see myself rather as a builder of little churches (for I am an architect) ; as one who has definite and very clear moral ideas which can partly be interpreted into buildings and partly into current daily life. But I do not see myself as a teacher. I admire the life and devotion of Saint Francis enormously, but I cannot see myself as setting out to follow him to the letter. I never see myself as a wandering preacher.

Intensely interested I am always in discussing things spiritual or cosmic, yet I cannot see myself arresting the flow of other people's lives to force the importance of these things into their minds.

To that extent I diverge from the character which is indicated in the scripts. And yet, I can never wholly be free from the influence of these writings. Try as I will to forget them, they remain. Sometimes rather like a dread responsibility, sometimes like a voice which is dear and beloved.

But they always have a living atmosphere to which I instantly respond, an atmosphere which is all their own.

" My son, my love is with ye so that ye are wrapped in it as in a mantle. . . ." Who could resist the charm of that ?

It may be asked, what is my attitude to such phrases in these writings as are all too generous to me. Some of these are instantly recognisable as errors and thus meet their end. With regard to others—parents on earth make similar phrases of endearment and one loves them for it, but one's estimate of the child remains pretty much what it was. I think that expresses my own attitude. I love Saint Francis for saying these things, but a sense of humour keeps me from loving myself any the more because he has said them. The whole atmosphere of the scripts is too holy (I can think of no better word) to engender personal emotions. In a way peculiar to themselves, they lift one to a place where aggrandisement withers and one sees only the love and beauty of " The Little Father."

Do I take it, then, that it is Francis who speaks ? My answer to that is : " Yes . . . ' I can no other.' "

I think it is quite probable that words, phrases, even ideas, may have become incorporated in the scripts which were never originated by Saint Francis ; nevertheless, as I see it, much is his and came from no other mind.

III

When I was twenty, someone gave me a book, the like of which I had never seen before. It was *The Little Flowers of Saint Francis*. No book I had ever read impressed me so much. The days and months which followed its discovery seem, on looking back, golden with their own wonderful light.

I do not think I was ever " psychic " in any but a spasmodic sense, and then only, for the most part, during my childhood and boyhood, but one night I decided to illustrate *The Little Flowers*, and after working for some hours on a drawing of Saint Francis praying in his " lonely place," I went to my bedroom and saw before

me, exquisite with the flash of diamond colour, Him
who appeared to Francis on Alvernia. I watched
amazed, until of necessity my hands covered my face.
The beauty of Christ and the beauty of Francis are
inseparable to me, and for some reason my own connection with Christ is through Saint Francis. Not until
twenty-six years had passed was I to know again the
beauty which filled those days.

In my very early years there were three of four occasions when there gleamed bright for a moment such
things as usually remain unseen. There are two which
were inexplicable at the time, but they came to have a
meaning later as psychic evidence grew. I was a child,
and I think it should be remembered that, in spite of
their vigour and gaiety, children are often more lonely
than they appear to be. I woke in the immensity of
night feeling small and solitary, until I saw, seated in an
arm-chair by the fire-place, a most wonderful lady.
There was no fear, only a most complete joy. I leapt
out of bed, set myself happily at her feet—and slept. The
morning found me with my head on the seat of the chair.

But there is a later vision contemporary with the
discovery of *The Little Flowers*. I was lying awake,
having just gone to bed, when, beyond the brass rail
at the foot of the bed, I saw six nuns. They looked
towards me and were discussing me. I have no memory
of hearing them, only of seeing their glances and movements. One who appeared to be a Superior came towards
me and, turning down the coverlet, looked into my face.
On rising she went back to the sisters and made an
affirmative gesture. After a final glance, all withdrew.

These things stirred deeps within me, emotions which
refuse to put themselves into words. I see them now as
through a golden vapour.

This very mist seems to have intention and meaning. Lately I have come to regard it as associated with ancient memory.

Certain places and people seem to me to live in that golden haze and, rightly or wrongly, I have come to accept that light as indicating a connection with a previous life. I have come also to accept both of the incidents just recorded as having a very direct connection with a previous life. This will be seen more clearly as the book proceeds.

IV

Twenty-six years after, all that of which I have written was buried beneath mountains of debris, buried and well-nigh forgotten. And when a stranger in the summer of 1928 turned to me in a friend's house and said : " What have you to do with Saint Francis ? " I replied, with more than a touch of laughter : " Why, nothing ! " But even as I spoke, I felt an element of doubt and, extraordinary as the remark was, I felt unable to dismiss it.

In a moment the lady returned to it : " He has been about all day and when I saw you I knew why he had come. . . . Surely there was something which happened in connection with him when you were a boy ? " It so chanced that further conversation was impossible, but I walked home impressed in spite of myself. I think that the chief reason why I took the matter seriously was the quality of the lady. She carried with her the aura of an ancient Irish family and no sentimentality could live for long in the bright twinkle of her humour. Self-absorption was not her weakness.

It need hardly be said, surely, that I perceived a psychic intention in her conversation. Although I had, at that time, met singularly few sensitives, the literature of psychical research had been familiar to me since I began by reading Myers about 1907. I had a fierce distrust of " big names " and a horror of supposed communications from historical figures.

The idea that Saint Francis should seek me appeared to me to border on the ridiculous. But it seemed, on reflection, in no way ridiculous that he should speak to this Irish lady. There was a simplicity and directness about her that made this, to my mind, remarkably possible. I had a feeling, which I have never since lost, that he was never very far from this unusual and unconventional woman.

Then and there began a small warfare which has never wholly left me. The strife is waged between two ideas : The consciousness of my own unsuitability, or unworthiness, or what you will. This is ranged against the evidence.

Supporting the evidence is a feeling which rises from a much deeper stratum than conscious argument. This feeling, or intuition, accepts Saint Francis without being particularly concerned with his greatness. It accepts him very much as a child accepts his own father. This intuition in me is very strong, and whatever objections my conscious mind has raised from time to time, that subconscious acceptance persists and has persisted throughout eleven very busy years.

That in my youth, when I drew Saint Francis on Alvernia, I had contact with him I began to suspect. I began also to feel that for some reason he was about to make a very definite approach.

V

It was here that the building of churches began. Hitherto, my work as an architect had been almost entirely secular. I had never designed a church. When, at the end of 1928, I was asked to build Hilborough Church, my response was pretty much what it would have been had I been asked to build a cinema. As the days passed, however, and the design began to evolve, a new feeling, hardly recognised then, began to creep in. I began to see that I could make this work not merely a well-executed commission, but an act of personal devotion. The words that came into my mind, I remember, were that I could make it a hymn to Almighty God.

There were, however, difficulties ahead.

The beginning of 1929 saw me with a high temperature and a very definite statement from four doctors that the next eight or nine months should be spent in the Alps. The church was designed as to the main structure, but innumerable details were still to be invented.

By February, I had arrived at a standstill, for the higher my temperature rose, the lower sank my power of design.

It was then that I received a caller. For a moment, I thought she was a stranger, and then, very gladly I recognised the lady, who, half a year before, had spoken to me of Saint Francis. Her name was Mrs. O'Connell. It appeared that she had heard of my illness and her business was to see if she could help me towards being healed. Although, since, healing has occasionally taken place through me, I still have no clear idea of what happens, but the power appears to come through the hand of the healer. That there was power that morning became obvious. But the crisis was not merely physical, it was spiritual.

" The monk in the brown cowl is here," said Mrs. O'Connell.

" But what is his name ? "

" He says that if you will allow him he will call himself your own brother."

" Allow him ! . . ."

Evidence ? There is none ; but that light I had felt, twenty-six years ago, filled the room. Here again was the strangeness that I had associated with Alvernia. The gold of it filled not the room merely, but my whole life. I write more than ten years after, but I know that no other day has ever been like that day, no other years have been like the years which followed.

A voice was chanting within my mind : " Not many wise men after the flesh, not many mighty, not many noble are called. But God hath chosen the foolish things. . . ."

Of course ! But though I might make Brother Juniper look staid by comparison, I had been called. That seemed very definite. What I had been called to do I did not know, but all the world was lit and gay with flowers on that bleak February day. The air was the air of the high Alps, the sun was the hot sun which wastes itself on the glaciers. And there was music.

I wish I could remember the exact date so that I could make it an anniversary to be kept, but I cannot remember it. It was, however, in February, 1929, that Saint Francis came, took my hand, and said : " Brother, we will now journey together." Not for one moment in the years since has that hand left mine.

VI

The immediate effect of all this was to make the building of Hilborough Church of the greatest importance. It became a symbol. The labour of it was indeed an offering. Whether it is a good building or not, it was the product of all my devotion. Not immediately, however, did I see that I shared with Francis the honour of building a church as my first definite spiritual effort. When I eventually entered Francis's first building, Saint Damian, just outside the walls of Assisi, it was again to feel intensely that same sense of golden light that came at the beginning of Hilborough Church.

It happens that occasionally I have been told that this church has an atmosphere. This I have felt myself, and I like to think that Francis put this there as his gift to me for doing as well as I could.

But if he has a peculiar grace in making gifts, he has a similar grace in receiving them. Not many days passed before I had thought of an idea connected with Hilborough Church which should stand as a memorial to his coming. This was to be a pool of water-lilies with running water and a small island-bath for birds in the centre. Presiding over all was to be a statue of Francis himself.

No human being knew of my intentions when Mrs. O'Connell paid her next visit, but before any healing was done I was thanked for my prospective gift to him, and on my asking " What gift ? " I had a full description of what I have written above.

There were, I knew, many difficulties to be overcome before this gift would be a completed work, the fact that Saint Francis was a Roman Catholic later proved to be one, but the only point which troubled me at the moment

was the cost. The church had so much to find for sheer
necessaries that I doubted much if they would welcome
an innovation which would seem to be a luxury to most
building committees. Half-way through the healing
treatment, Mrs. O'Connell said : " The little Brother
wishes me to say that the money for the gift will be
found in five weeks."

I was about to depart for Switzerland, but before
leaving I explained to a rather cold committee my
proposals regarding the pool. As I expected, the idea
received no encouragement.

I was in the Alps for six weeks. The first remark I
heard from an official on my return was that the pool had
proved unexpectedly popular, and the money for it was
already raised.

For about eighteen months I kept closely in touch with
Mrs. O'Connell, and at intervals, mostly unexpectedly,
I received messages either by note or by word of mouth.
One day, indeed when I was particularly forlorn, there
came a pot of honey " which," said a note, " the little
Brother asked me to send as you are downcast."

VII

Mrs. O'Connell lived a dozen miles away in the heart
of a wood ; we met only occasionally, and she knew little
of my personal life, so that many of her notes were
peculiarly striking. One day I was evolving a new
church in a rather casual way, but gradually it assumed
quite new and, as I thought, interesting lines. Actually
I was in Switzerland at this time. Two days after, I
received these words : " It is that the Brother Francis
would speak to his brother Lorenzo in the mountains.

He is dear to the Little Poor Man. Tell him that his dream will be fulfilled yet about the House of Prayer that he and Francis will bring together. . . . Tell him that the trees already are full-grown by which the little House will stand."

Two years later I was asked to build a church at Inglewell, in Surrey. The sketch I had made became the basis of the design. When I visited the site there were full-grown trees along the front, and these still stand.

As time went on the healing was successful. How successful I can say in a few words. Serious pulmonary trouble was diagnosed by my own doctor. This was confirmed by an X-ray consultant locally. A few weeks after it was again confirmed separately by two French specialists in Switzerland, both using X-rays. This was during February and March. In June all temperature had departed, and although I have since had another illness it had no relation to this, and, ten years after, I can say that I have had no sign of a return.

VIII

Most people will understand how difficult it is to accept the idea, during each of the twenty-four hours of every day, that a Being like Saint Francis has made himself one's own especial friend. My greatest help was to remember his attitude to the men he met when he lived on earth; his sweetness to those suffering from moral or physical infirmity, and how in sheer joy of heart he became a beggar so that he might be one with the outcast and the leper.

But, even so, there were days when belief burned dim.

Working alone one day—actually, I believe, I was designing the pulpit of Hilborough Church—I received the impression that he was in the room with me. I stopped drawing and considered. Was I involved in a hopeless piece of vanity and self-deception ? Why, of all people, should he come to me ?

I turned and put the case to him. Speaking aloud, I explained how dark our minds were here, how limited ; and how difficult was any genuine belief in the Unseen, how especially difficult it was to accept the idea of his interest in me. I then begged of him some proof.

" Let me," I said, " be asked to the house of Mrs. O'Connell. Let her then be made to speak for you. Cause her to use some special word, say the word ' Light,' over and over again, so that it will be clear that there is intention behind it. Particularly would I ask to see the birds about you, if that be possible."

That ended the request, and I continued my work in the unresponsive silence.

The responses of Francis come in their own time and in their own way, but they come. My work next day was interrupted by the arrival of the friend in whose house I had met Mrs. O'Connell months before. He and his wife were calling on her ; would I come ?

It was a wonderful June day, and on arrival we sat in a garden house which was in the very midst of a wood. Tea being over, the three or four other people stepped out into the trees. I was asked to remain.

" The Little Brother is here," said my hostess, " he has something to say to you." There was a pause, and then, hesitating a little, she said : " The words for you are Light, Life, and Love. He says them over and over again. ' Tell him,' he says, ' that light will come to him ; especially would I say that light will come.' "

Those words were repeated in many forms and then Mrs. O'Connell turned to me and said : " He wishes us to walk to those beech trees."

Before us was one of those wonderful glades which make the more picturesque centres of all great forests. It was made, mainly, of beeches with a natural lawn in their midst.

When we stood in this silent little chapel, it was obvious that my friend was in trance. We stood perfectly still. Presently a bird dropped like a spent arrow at our feet. This was immediately followed by a second and a third. Birds slid down the air from all quarters ; some stood fluttering on the ground, others alighted on the low delicate boughs around us. I never counted them, but I have always thought that there were about fourteen, there might have been one or two more. It is quite likely that they were not all visible.

" This," said a whispered voice from my friend's lips, " is only a greeting. It is difficult." There was a moment's silence, then her eyes opened and, as though at a sign, the birds departed.

IX

I do not think that even my own mind made any immediate comment to itself on the events of that afternoon. It was years before I discussed the matter with any human being. I had had a great shock. We do not know the depth and extent of our own doubts until they are shattered. There was a mind behind these manifestations and it was deliberate and purposeful. I could not conceive that this master of practical imagination and vigorous spirituality was merely entertaining me.

If what I had seen had really happened, what was expected of me? It seemed obvious at that moment that the intentions, the standards of life, would have to be reviewed. It was becoming clear that the objective could no longer be my own interests alone. If this was indeed Saint Francis, something profound was afoot. It was urgent that I discover my own responsibilities and carry them out.

There were many happenings, such as I have written down, connected with Mrs. O'Connell, and altogether, except for a few isolated cases, these lasted for about eighteen months. The last note from her which I can trace as belonging to this period contains these words, quoted as having been spoken to her: " Tell him that his brother Francis is full of love and joy for him. Tell him that Francis is very near to him; very near when the earth turns itself to the light of the morning."

The particular quality in these words is typical of all the hundreds of messages which have come to me bearing his name.

x

The next eighteen months, that is from about June, 1930, to January, 1932, have no ordered sequence of communications. Sometimes I was tempted to think that a very remarkable period had closed. But before I record the two or three isolated happenings belonging to these months I must touch upon the discovery of a new friend who, until her death in 1934, led me by her gifts to a much larger conception of life.

Alice Mortley did most of her work anonymously. She it was who wrote the little book called, *Christ in You,* which, to her great amazement, had a world-wide sale. I have not been able to follow its career for some years, but well before her death it was translated into five languages. There are other books, one of which is called *Spiritual Reconstruction*, and there were many articles. But the wonderful effect of Alice Mortley was not created by her books, but by herself. There was an extraordinarily simple power about her; it was not easy to know of what this consisted. She lived a solitary life, for most of the time I knew her she was an invalid and was far from being accessible. If one needed help to achieve an ambition, however innocent, Alice Mortley was not to be found. If it was spiritual help that was needed, she was at one's side and like a rock.

On two or three occasions I had the clearest possible evidence that she knew, quite definitely, details of situations connected with my life, or of actions I had taken, which she could not possibly have known normally. I well remember receiving from her an envelope containing a correspondence card. On the card was written these words and no others: " This is your Everest : keep your vows." I had not seen her for some months, nor had she, nor indeed, anyone else, any means of knowing normally that I was passing through a crisis.

Whether she could command this clairvoyance, I do not know. In any case, she would be the last person to use it without high motive. That she could command it where there would be spiritual advantage to all concerned, I can well believe. To call Alice Mortley a psychic would be to give her a negative and insufficient title. A psychic awaits communications from a level higher than her own. Alice Mortley had the spiritual development which would permit her to gather her own harvest by entering the higher levels herself.

In a room full of people you might not see her at first, but once you had seen her you would see no one else.

A friend, a public figure of great talent, but who was by no means given to easy admirations, once asked me if I had ever met Alice Mortley. I said that I had, and that apparently he had. Would he tell me then in what way she impressed him. With genuine emotion, he said : " Temple, I was awe-inspired." And no man I have ever met could use words more intelligently.

Alice Mortley chose, usually, to be part of a grey background, but without effort she could suddenly suggest the tremendous powers of hidden realms.

I am not sure what constitutes friendship. If it means the right of entry into another person's life, I cannot claim friendship with her. One would think twice before claiming any possessive rights in Alice Mortley's life, nor did she claim similar rights in any degree whatsoever herself. I have known few other persons similarly constituted.

What does surprise me is the fact that between June, 1929, and October 26th, 1934, when she died, she wrote to me thirty-one letters, each of which is precious. I had no idea until I counted them that there were so many.

But in June, 1929, I knew nothing of these things. Both her name and her work were unknown to me. And although her entrance into my life was in this month, it was not until after that I felt the full force of her peculiar genius.

XI

In that wonderful June some recently discovered friends were driving me to Marlborough College. In the exquisite woodland of Savernake the car drew up for us to make a picnic lunch. I had been seated in the front and had only been barely introduced to the lady who had sat behind with my friend's wife.

At lunch, under the great trees, I was placed beside this unknown lady who proved to be Alice Mortley. She immediately turned to me with a smile and asked if I knew anything of psychical matters. This, I think, was merely a convenient opening remark, for I have now no doubt whatever that she would know not only that I was acquainted with psychical matters, but precisely to what extent I was acquainted with them.

However, such things could not be known to me at this time, and I assured her that I was quite familiar with most of the forms of evidence.

She then said : " I asked to come on this journey as I have to tell you two or three things.

" First, it is very important how you live, just now especially. I am sure you know of the Grail. Let me tell you that you may have the glory of the Grail in that church you are building. The choice is with you."

I cannot hope to put down here precisely how much I was moved by her words. They seemed to have authority behind them, and they swept me headlong into humility.

" I think," she went on, " you know who is leading you. There is a true personal link between you, almost like that between human lovers, but much stronger. You are as one sometimes. And the love pours from each to each. You will help many by this mutual love, it goes out to all kindred spirits.

" Be quite sure that your work is under high guidance. This, in your case, is especially true, as one sees that you have belonged to an old Guild of Abbey Builders. You have often done splendid work as a craftsman, but this last work has been given to you as a Master Mason.

"Rest all you can; later you will be given back many memories of previous lives. The angels are with you. God bless you."

She finished quite abruptly and turned to her lunch. To say that I was impressed is to speak foolishly. I was overwhelmed.

Alice Mortley did not return again to her message. The rest of the day was spent as four friendly and normal people would spend a blue day in happy surroundings.

XII

With the building of Hilborough Church, it was inevitable that I made several new friends and some scores of friendly acquaintances.

Mr. and Mrs. Carey were not known well to me. One day Mrs. Carey, meeting me among the shops, asked me if I would look in to see her husband who was ill and would like to speak to me. Shortly after, I found myself with him and discovered him to be very ill indeed. He had some internal trouble which the doctors regarded as being permanent. It had originated, I think, in the war. Mr. Carey was not difficult to talk to, indeed, I was drawn to him. Presently he came to some mental decision, for he asked quite suddenly : " Why did you put the statue of Saint Francis in front of Hilborough Church ? "

I hesitated a moment, for this question pointed to the sort of conversation I preferred, on the whole, to avoid. Then I said: " Because I thought he helped me to build it."

" Do you think that such Beings are about us ? "

" Yes, I do. But I think I would like to say that

probably they have their own great lives to live, and they will not do for us what we should do for ourselves."

" Do you think they care for us ? "

" That is exactly what I do think. And also, I think that their love is, well, indescribably beautiful."

" Do you think that Saint Francis could make me well ? "

When he said that, there came upon me that sense of golden light I had known before, and the feeling of great beauty and affection. It was as though Saint Francis himself was within me and I was humble before him.

" Carey," I said, " I know so little of how these things work. But I do know this, if they will, and if you will, you can be healed."

In a moment, I knew for a certainty that the ineffable love which filled me had poured into him. It was a matter of seconds and then, I remember, we discussed Glastonbury and the discoveries Bligh Bond had made there.

Three days later I met Mrs. Carey, who asked me gaily what I had done to her husband.

" How is he ? " I asked.

" He is better, and when I say better, I mean he is cured and is usually ravenously hungry."

The cure, I found, was not only true, but it remained true and complete.

A very similar healing took place on one other occasion, and, so far as I know, only on one, and the trouble was equally serious. I know now very little more than I did then. Both cases happened nine years ago as I write. In both, the trouble was organic ; in both, I was very conscious of the " power " and that it was not my own power.

XIII

The first case led to a situation where my personal limitations were made very clear. And as the matter is interesting for that reason, and as also it touches on the genius of Alice Mortley, I will record it briefly.

One night towards midnight, a knock came on my door, and I was told that Mr. Carey wished to see me. Slipping on a dressing-gown, I went down to find a man so apologetic that any irritation I felt at this late call was instantly removed.

It appeared that Carey's brother-in-law, Peter Ferris, a very young man, was desperately ill.

"It comes to this," said Carey, "will you do for Peter what you did for me?"

"Now, there you go headlong, Carey," I said, "it is difficult to make it quite clear that I really and truly did nothing for you. This is not a graceful figure of speech, it is dead true. All I did was to act as a kind of lightning-conductor."

"Very good," he said, "will you be a lightning-conductor for Peter?"

"I will tell you what I will do, and it is all I can do. I will go and see him. Should the same Power wish to operate as operated with you—well and good. But do realise that there may be no results of any kind."

A time was fixed, indeed, it was arranged that each day I should call at eleven o'clock and six o'clock.

When I saw the young boy lying silent and barely conscious my heart went out to him. As I placed my hand on his head he smiled, and I prayed with all the force of my will for his recovery.

In two days he was slightly better. On the third day,

at midday, a letter awaited me in Alice Mortley's handwriting. It said :

"MY DEAR BROTHER,
        "What are you attempting ?   Come and see me.
                                                "A. M."

Alice Mortley was now an invalid herself and was completely separated from my own world. As she was so difficult to meet, I very gladly availed myself of what to me was a command.

"What are you trying to do ? " she said at once when I entered.   "Are you attempting to heal someone ? "

"Yes."

"Is it God's will that he should be healed, or is it just yours ? "

I am obliged to say that that simple question brought my thoughts to a very sudden focus.   Had I felt that golden sense of another Power ?   I had not.   Was I personally trying to force the issue ?   There was only one answer.

"My dear Alice Mortley," I said, "I am ashamed to say that I am endeavouring to impose my will."

"Yes.   Are you aware that if you succeed you will be incurring responsibilities that you cannot very well meet ? "

"I am afraid that I did not realise that."

"Brother, you must never intrude.   When your work is required the fact will always be made quite clear to you.   You are holding this boy back.   When are you going again ? "

"At six o'clock this evening."

"Then go with God.   Stand by the boy and release him in your mind.   Say : ' God's will be done,' he will then be free to go.   To-night, as you sleep, you will help

him across the difficult country. That is what you were
wanted to do ; you mistook your work."

This was the authentic Alice Mortley bringing me
back to spiritual sanity.

How very easy it is to slip aside into personal desires.
Peter died that night, and that same night I slept deeply.

I have as much scientific curiosity as anyone I know,
but never could I have asked Alice Mortley how she knew
all that was implied by that conversation.

XIV

The further life took me, the more anxious I was to
gain some insight into the structure of the worlds. It
was obvious that there must be gigantic processes at
work of which we see only a small part of the results.
So far as I could see, there would probably be principles
at work of which neither science nor religion, as usually
understood, knew anything. It seemed likely, too, that
with so much achieved, there were, somewhere, great
Orders of Craftsmen, Architects, Builders, and Engineers,
each with their staffs ; Designers and Constructors who
had worked through æons of time, until we had the
maze of achievement which we saw about us.

If God delegated work, to whom did he delegate it ?

At one point in my quest, I became acquainted with
the work of Dion Fortune and with her Fraternity. Her
books and lectures gave me at least a hypothetical framework, a cosmic doctrine. So far as I am able to
judge, it is a good one ; one's own experience fits
reasonably into it, and this is the only method open to
most of us of assessing the value of any doctrine. Schuré
and Rudolf Steiner, with their vivid sense of colour,

helped me to see Dion Fortune's scheme live. But a dozen great writers gave me a wider view.

Attached to Dion Fortune's Fraternity, was a Mr. Loveday with whom I soon became acquainted. As he was to stay in Glastonbury during part of the summer of 1930, I went also, and for three weeks we held conversations lasting for several hours each day. This gave me an insight into the possibilities of the Cosmos such as I could never have come by alone.

During our conversations it was natural that I should tell Loveday at least some of the details connected with Mrs. O'Connell and Alice Mortley.

The Fraternity had a little hostel on the slopes of Glastonbury Tor. One afternoon during August I was seated on the very wide balcony which runs along the front of the building. Below was the steep side of the Tor and an orchard of apple trees. Presently, Loveday came out to where I was seated. With him was a lady who was a stranger to me.

After the introductions Loveday said : " Will you tell this lady about Saint Francis ? " And then, speaking to the lady : " Temple will make this very interesting for you."

I hadn't at all welcomed Loveday's suggestion. This particular subject I do not speak easily on. However, I drew up a chair for the lady and noticed that she looked frail and there was a suspicion of recent trouble. At the outset I was very clumsy and full of hesitations. I was pausing again for a phrase, when, from the apple trees below, out shot what appeared to be a brown bullet. To my great surprise, it passed close to my face and perched behind me on the top rail of my chair. It was a wren.

For a moment I was amazed, and then, realising that it

might suddenly take fright and hurt itself, I rose, held out my hand, and said: "Come along, Jenny." The wren hopped on to my finger and I walked to the front of the balcony with it.

"Now," I said, "away!" And back shot the bullet to the trees below. This incident certainly made conversation on Saint Francis easier.

In November, 1936, a little more than six years after, I happened to be sitting for the first time with Geraldine Cummins in her charming little workroom in Chelsea. Her hand had just written the name of Francis, when there followed these words (apparently to Miss Cummins):

"I am glad to meet my brother . . . I want to call to his remembrance the signs I have given to him in past years, then he will know his guardian."

(Then to me.) "Do you remember a hostelry and a bird that came near and perched upon your chair? And then it came shyly and settled upon your arm? I was behind you then. That wren saw me. . . ."

There followed other interesting points, but their place is later in the book. If the word "finger" is substituted for "arm," the description of a little event that I had ceased thinking of for years, is exact.

XV

Towards the end of 1931, practically nothing of a psychic nature had come to me for about twelve months.

Plenty of time this for the mind to review every conceivable explanation. Telepathy and the Subconscious like twin thieves, stole silently into view, hesitated on hearing of the wren and retired on being told of the gathering around Mrs. O'Connell. But the civilised mind is almost incurably materialistic. Even a Dean has said that miracles can be relegated to the sphere of pious opinion. What wonder then if I began to think of further inquiry when, in the first days of 1932, a friend asked me if I had ever met Hester Dowden.

I had not met her. All I knew of her was her work in connection with Glastonbury and her Oscar Wilde scripts. She had no possible knowledge of me. Here was a cultured woman, the daughter of a distinguished scholar. She was also mediumistic. The combination appealed to me.

A letter to Miss Estelle Stead quickly brought about an anonymous appointment, and on January 30th, 1932, at 3.30 p.m., I was being shown into her beautiful drawing-room in Cheyne Gardens.

She was quiet, rather grave. Almost indifferently she said as she drew her pencils and paper towards her: "There is a strong thirteenth-century atmosphere about you."

She showed no disposition to ask questions, and I shall never forget the strange thrill I had when, two minutes later, her hand had written the word "Francesco."

Since that day, I have come to know the details of his life very intimately and to have a friendly acquaintance with every stone in Assisi. The name "Francesco" is now probably more familiar to me than "Francis." At that time, however, "Francis of Assisi" was the name by which I always thought of him, and the word "Francesco" came unexpectedly.

But to return to the beginning of the sitting. After a short discussion between herself and her control Johannes, a ouija-board was put between us. Both Mrs. Dowden and I placed a hand upon it.

Mrs. Dowden mentioned that there were a lot of brothers about.

" Do you mean my brothers ? " I asked.

" Monks," she replied briefly.

At that moment the traveller moved so violently, that my hand slipped off and only towards the end of what was apparently a sentence did I catch up with it again.

Mrs. Dowden came to my help. " It spelled out : ' Your own brother.' Had you a brother a monk ? "

I made a non-committal answer. To start some sort of conversation, I asked : " What kind of work do I do ? "

The instantaneous reply was : " Architecture."

" Thank you, can you put it more definitely ? "

" Churches."

All that was spelled out so rapidly that I was unable to follow the pointer.

XVI

It was here that the ouija-board was abandoned as being too slow, and Mrs. Dowden took paper and pencil to write. The communication began in the middle of a sentence :

" . . . the church of which I speak was not entirely built out of thine own mind. Ye had help from our side, from those who lived in the thirteenth century."

" Who were those who helped ? "

" They were not builders themselves, they were those who saw buildings with the inner eye. . . . I have tried many times to draw ye to a possible opening of the door, to the knowledge of what the work ye do means."

" You speak of churches and of my work. Is the designing of churches then my work ? "

"It is. The three who guide ye in England are all ecclesiastical."

"But let me know who is speaking."

It was here that Mrs. Dowden wrote rather more slowly and emphatically the word "Francesco." At this point, I took great pains to show no recognition. After a moment's consideration, I said :

"Have I met you before ? "

"Yea," said the script, "ye have, and ye have seen me surrounded with flowers. Ye have been to my native town, ye were very happy there and felt ye had come home. Ye belong to me and I to ye. I am closer to ye than any of the others. Ye have seen my lilies, my brother, many times. . . . I was pleased that ye gave thy brother a gift, but the real gift ye give is the building of the churches."

Mrs. Dowden, who had no idea of how this script moved me, here showed a great desire to know if I could be taught to write automatically ; a gift I have, curiously, never coveted. But the current, which had been turned aside for a moment by these questions, leapt back with the words :

"Beato Lorenzo. Go on and with prayer. Be as simple as a child and marvels will be granted ye.

"Always remember, that the body is but a casket that contains precious essence which must never be polluted by lust, or love of what is material. So long as the essence is pure, the lines on which thy work is done are pure also. Ye will build several churches."

"Do you know my church at Garstone ? " I asked.

"Ah ! that is a little chapel I will help ye with, as it is dearer to me than the greater churches. It is the Chapel of the Fioretti. Ye will make this beautiful for my flowers."

At this point the power failed, and after I had made arrangements to see Mrs. Dowden again, I left.

XVII

There are one or two points connected with this sitting upon which I wish to remark.

The first is, that I have slightly condensed the script, but I have deleted nothing which would alter essential values.

The second is concerning the name Lorenzo, which is, of course, the Italian form of Laurence. Mrs. Dowden, at this time, had no knowledge of my name, nor had I referred in any way to the name Lorenzo which had been used previously by Mrs. O'Connell, and which has been used since by a dozen mediums who had no knowledge of me.

The third point is the reference to the lily pond. This, which I had built in Hilborough eighteen months before, was not, of course, known to the medium.

The fourth point is the insistence upon the designing of churches as being my work.

This had a real interest for me. In sittings with Mrs. Dowden, and later with other mediums, it has been referred to over and over again, and particularly during one with Mrs. Dowden on May 7th.

Let me explain the situation from the standpoint of this world.

I had been an architect for a good many years and had erected about one thousand buildings. All but one of these had been secular. Houses, shops, garages, a school, a hotel; year in and year out, I had built such things. I had finished Hilborough Church during June, 1930.

I had been asked to build a small church, by no means an important one as ordinarily understood, at Garstone. On the best reckoning, the proportion of churches to other buildings was thus two in a thousand, or one-fifth of one per cent.

On May 7th, 1932, this question was referred to again. Many will remember the period around 1932. Building, among other forms of production, seemed to have come to a natural and final end ; and I thought and said that the references to my designing more " Houses of Prayer " were the outcome of faulty judgment.

Quickly and emphatically following this thought, through the hand of Mrs. Dowden, came these words :
" Ye need not care or be worried about these Houses that ye are to build. Of a sudden will the work come on ye and ye will find it hard to do all that is required of ye."

Practically nothing but a letter or two from church building committees followed that for two years. About October, 1934, a veritable avalanche came upon me. The words just quoted were more than merely fulfilled. Indeed, within a year, I used to fear to go to my office in case another committee should have written. Letters from about seventy towns and villages came to me during a period of a few months. As I write in midsummer, 1939, there have been somewhere over thirty church contracts completed, and there are about twenty more in various stages of being planned and many not yet begun.

I have written fully on this point because here was a very material result following a prediction which no living person could normally have made. I, least of all. Every medium I have seen since has referred to " your churches."

One of the later of such allusions followed the reference

to the " wren incident " at Glastonbury in the script of
November 14th, 1936, by Geraldine Cummins. The
words are :

" Ye are my brother on earth, set to carry out the task
of raising churches to our Blessed Lord and Master.

" Other signs I gave ye were the demands from the
people of thy land to build churches. Is that not so ? "

XVIII

It is hardly necessary to point out that Saint Francis
was becoming not merely my daily companion, but my
inseparable brother. " Ye are lit with my light, and
surrounded with my radiance, for I am within ye and
without," wrote the hand of Ethel Green two years later.

There were no moments in any day when I was not
conscious of him. He shared my joys, my troubles,
and my sins. And it was here that the crux came. No
reproof ever healed a spiritual defect. But love that
knows no blame, no pride, is a powerful and rare force.
The feeling that I grew to have for this indwelling
brotherhood passes such words as I am able to use.

A clergyman discussing Saint Francis with me, once
said : " Delightful, of course, but how little he had to
give which would help us in the difficulties of our own
day." I felt then and I feel now, that he had all that was
necessary to enable us to meet any difficulties of any day.
And if it is conceivable to imagine a world of Saints
Francis, it is inconceivable to imagine any great difficulties
ever arising in it.

His unwavering affection, which never by any chance
deserted me, gradually rebuilt me. " My son, be at
peace," again it is the script of Ethel Green, " for I am

with ye and my hand leadeth ye by night and day. My life groweth within ye and controlleth the desires of thine heart and the thoughts of thy mind. Atom by atom is being built within ye the new man who shall attain . . ."

Advice is easy, shocked reproof is simple, both surely, are useless. To rebuild a soul needs all the patience, all the love and nobility of which any Being is capable. It needs endurance and the power to give of the essential Self. The shame of any falling back bore not merely on me, but on him.

XIX

As the days passed, the old question arose and demanded an answer : " Why me ? " Here with me was my friend in the dawn. Here was my friend when night enclosed the world. Nor can I even hint at the exquisite relationship, the glimmering, soundless Presence, the fire within the bush. But again : " Why me ? " Had I, seven hundred years ago, seen him passing by ? Did I know that brown cowl ? Vanity would have been satisfied in me had I been told that I had even touched that brave gown, so sombre, so gay. But there were deeps below vanity in this. There was that tendency in discussion to say : " But I *knew* him." Did I not know the very soul of that man who could love and bless even as the fire approached to sear him ?

On February 12th, while I was with Mrs. Dowden, came the inevitable question : " Did I ever know you on earth ? "

" Ye ask me a very simple question," he said. " Why should I choose you and come to you, were you not of my own Brotherhood ?

" You were with us long ago in the Little Town. And you are the one that was my especial friend and confidant in the Brotherhood, on whom I often laid my griefs."

There was my answer. . . . I had known him . . . his griefs.

The laugh and the love which sprang out of the shadows when I was perplexed . . . were these indeed, in very deed, the old memory bridging death and re-birth ? Such thoughts were woven into the very fabric of the work I did in those days. And, out of sheer weari-ness of the mental questions which followed, I would shut the door on them and refuse to discuss them even with myself.

But again, on February 12th : " Francesco is speaking to his brother Lorenzo. I wish that you should under-stand that your eyes are being opened to what is about you, below you, and above you. Be not haughty that this is so, let it come as a flower that opens in the sun."

That was sound. I had no difficulty in accepting it, for in my bones I could feel knowledge creeping in. Not new knowledge, old knowledge, old atmospheres, grey old laughter, which was yet fresh with the childhood of the soul.

xx

But who was Lorenzo ? There is no Lorenzo in the Fioretti. No Lorenzo is reported to have climbed with Saint Francis the steeps of Assisi.

On February 20th, with Mrs. Dowden, I put that as a question.

" Francesco speaks to you as Lorenzo," came the reply, " but in the Fioretti the whole name was not given. The name I gave you in religion, was Leo."

Leo. . . . "The name I gave you was Leo." . . .
Here was something I dared hardly repeat even to
myself. Frankly, I left it. There is an arrangement in
my mind, I feel sure that others will know what I mean,
by which any new and astounding statement gets shut into
an interior cupboard and left while the business of life
rides on.

If there was any truth in this, let it appear by itself.
Still I would tell Mrs. Dowden that this new name was
a shock.

On Tuesday, February 23rd, three days after, I
received a note from Mrs. Dowden and a small script :

" To my dear brother Lorenzo, Francesco speaks. He
sees with a smile the confusion which he has caused.
The brother's name that will be his always and throughout all spheres is Lorenzo. That is the name that was his
from the first incarnation on earth. After he had come
into my Order I gave him the name Leo ; and this was
my gift to him. So is Leo his name permanently together
with Lorenzo. You may call him Lorenzo Leo, for these
names shall be his through all eternity."

Mrs. Dowden had taken the trouble to sit alone, and I
appreciated her kindness. She had, moreover, made it
clear in a covering note that she accepted the general
truth of the script herself.

XXI

But was ever a serious and modest inquirer placed in
a more trying situation ? This friendship between
Francis and Leo which culminated on Alvernia and
which, even when I was twenty, I had recognised as

being one of the most lovely things which had ever blessed a rather indifferent world, this, I was told, was not an external happening, but was a part of my own life. The love Leo had for Francis was my love. The love Francis had for Leo was for me. I had always recoiled from communications which were stated to have come from the distinguished dead, and my trouble was that now I was asked to become an historical figure. And it is hardly surprising, knowing the chances of error in any psychic communication, if the human side of me shrank.

Nevertheless, below that somewhat self-conscious attitude, there would always remain the peculiar love that I had for Saint Francis. This has no variability, it has stood immovable against the onslaughts of time.

There are more people who have an affectionate interest in Saint Francis than there are those who love him. But where I have, in writers and others, met the authentic love, some voice deep within myself has said : " There goes one of the Brothers."

Still, this was undoubtedly a matter to be shut into the mental cupboard. It was a point which could hardly be proved. I decided that there was one possible way of treating it. Let it be an impersonal matter entirely, so that proof or disproof would be of merely intellectual interest. With regard to my own moral conduct, I could always endeavour to act as though I had been, and indeed still was, the intimate of the Little Brother.

At the point where I had satisfactorily dismissed the whole matter Mrs. O'Connell returned from Italy where she had been for some time. None of the above perplexities were known to her. I am not sure that she knows of them now. But even as I shook her hand she said : " He has something for you." Her little queer trance came again as she stood. She lifted my hand and, with her finger, wrote on the palm, slowly and very clearly, the word " LEO."

" That was the Little Brother," she said.

XXII

A rather quaint happening occurred about this time, or rather, just before. It is, I think, worth recording. It will be remembered how, a little while ago, I quoted the script as saying that my eyes were " being opened to what is about you, below you, and above you."

Being with Mrs. Dowden on March 4th I asked that a message might be sent to me through Mrs. O'Connell who was in Italy, and who would be about that time in Assisi.

Francesco replied : " I did send a message which ye shall have soon and which will give ye joy and a little surprise."

A letter in fact awaited me as the words were written.

It was dated Assisi, March 1st, 1932. There was a postscript : " Tuesday. To-day as I finish this note, Francis himself sends this word to you, his brother :

' We are a watchful bodyguard before, behind, above, beneath, beside you ! ' "

The joy was in the message, the surprise was in the phrasing. Surely the similarity between the two communications was intentional ?

XXIII

To revert to the name " Leo." In the end I came, provisionally at least, to accept it. Partly because of the insistence of the gentle figure in the shadows, and partly because a little later the scripts took an entirely new turn. New vistas opened, and to hang upon one item of evidence seemed to hold up some very definite purpose behind the writings.

Alice Mortley, whose influence upon me was very strong, completely accepted the matter. About this time, also, I met a new friend, a Mrs. Forrest, who was to give me a new view upon one or two details of the Franciscan life. She took the name as a matter of course. Six years after she had accepted the name, Mrs. Forrest chanced to attend a Spiritualist meeting in London. Both hall and medium were strange to her, and, I may say, equally unknown to me.

It was the spring of 1939, and, after an unsuccessful operation of a year before, I was extremely ill. The medium asked her across the hall if she knew one called " Leo " who was ill. Mrs. Forrest made it clear that she did. The medium then said that a lady called Clare, who was with one named Francis, wished her to tell Leo that his pain would soon be healed.

When I received this message its evidential value intrigued me, but my illness was so severe and had been so prolonged that I doubted its correctness. Nevertheless, two months after, a further operation was advised and this cured me of two and a half years of pain.

XXIV

If I give now an outline of such further evidence as I obtained, the matter can then be left.

After the whole episode had come to a climax, that is when the one hundred and sixty-fourth script had been written, a sort of perversity drove me to try and obtain contradictions.

On April 13th, 1934, I arranged with the British College of Psychic Science for an anonymous sitting with Miss Francis. The choice of this particular medium rested on nothing except that even should she discover my name, it would mean nothing to her. I entered the building expecting to hear news of somewhat indefinite relatives, but within a quarter of an hour I was a very surprised man. I would record the whole sitting here, but that I wish at the moment not to introduce new points of departure.

The name "Leo" was one of the earliest points brought up. This was introduced immediately after the control had said: "You, Brother, belong to Saint Francis.

"You see, surely you see," said the control, "that when you did the work with Saint Francis you bore that name."

The whole sitting was a crowded and interesting hour and left me very thoughtful, for, although Miss Francis knew nothing of me, all the essential details given to me during the previous five years were referred to, the name "Leo" being an almost minor instance. Many new and impressive points were introduced, which later were confirmed without suggestion from me, by other mediums.

That same month, that is on April 30th, 1934, I was fortunate enough to obtain another sitting with Miss Francis under the same conditions. I must make it very clear that I had given no clue as to my name. Neither Laurence nor Lorenzo had yet been mentioned either by or before Miss Francis. I asked quite abruptly: "Who was Lorenzo?"

" Why," laughed the control, " who should know but you ! "

" I knew him ? "

" He was very close to you in your own church last night." (It was true that I had been in " my own church " the night before.)

" Then *I* am Lorenzo ? "

" Of course, Lorenzo is your permanent name."

" Then," said I, feigning ignorance, " who *is* Leo ? " (for the control had been addressing me by that name).

" Oh, ho ! " he said, " Leo is that part of you that incarnated with Saint Francis."

When one considers the number of ideas embodied in that one statement, the chances against two strangers like Mrs. Dowden and Miss Francis arriving normally at the same thought are considerable.

XXV

From Helen Hughes who, until she sat with me in July, 1936, had never accepted reincarnation ; from Grace Cooke, from Geraldine Cummins, from Alice Mortley, Ethel Green, Mrs. Dowden, Mrs. O'Connell, and from six or seven other mediums, private or public, I obtained the selfsame story without hesitation and often against very careful suggestions made by myself to create other ideas.

" I will speak to thee through others of my children . . ." Francesco said through Ethel Green at a later date. " For at no time will I leave ye in doubt, but proof upon proof shall be laid before ye."

The very first words of Geraldine Cummins's script, after the name Francesco Bernardone had been given, were these : " My brother, I am come to remind you of our bond. Leo . . . speak to me, Leo."

Details of an incident which impressed me as much as any, because of its curious indirectness, were given to me in a letter.

A group of ladies, only one of whom (not the medium) is known to me, had recently been sitting for psychic development. One of the number is intensely medium-istic and is usually controlled by a Chinaman, whose name is Dr. Amenchu. Only a limited number of her friends know of her psychic gifts, but she is the natural centre of the group. Occasionally there are apports.

From the member with whom I am acquainted I received the following letter on the morning of December 17th, 1938 :

" I hope you will forgive me for troubling you with this letter, but something has happened which interests me enormously and I feel I must report it.

" Dr. Amenchu woke me at 6 o'clock this morning, giving me a name he has tried to give me many times during the sittings and which I could not understand. He finds names very difficult and cannot give them clearly, but he was most anxious to give this one, and was very much distressed when I couldn't understand.

" ' *I have* to give it,' he said, ' there are those who want me to give the name : Illego, Illeo, Ellego . . .' He tried many times until someone in the circle (being helpful) suggested that the name was Inigo.

" ' No,' I said, ' I know no one of that name.'

" Dr. Amenchu was most worried. ' No, no, not quite that,' he said. ' Do you not understand ? '

" ' But I don't know anyone with a name like that,' I said.

" Someone else made various suggestions, but in the end we had to abandon it. Dr. Amenchu, however, was obviously far from satisfied and so was I.

" Then this morning, I woke suddenly and heard his voice, saying, ' Ell-i-o, L-E-O.' Then, of course, I understood. . . ."

Allowing for the final discovery to be a subconscious uprush in the waking state, it is difficult to understand how telepathy could have caused the curious little incident.

And so I accepted the name . . . provisionally.

XXVI

But if my mind hesitated to accept the name " Leo," what shall be said of what follows ?

The passages in Mrs. Dowden's scripts of February 20th and March 4th, 1932, from which I am about to quote, compel one to consider the possibility of individuals being not so completely separated from one another as they appear. One might imagine them as a group of islands, each to the eye a distinct and separate domain with its own characteristics, and yet below sea-level all are united in a common parent earth.

It may be that the phrase used by Christ : " I am the vine, ye are the branches," is, on some level more literally true than is usually understood.

Briefly, one branch may bear many lesser branches through all of which the same spiritual life-blood flows. The lesser branches would partake of the essence of the parent branch and would be tinctured by its own particular quality.

Some idea of this sort seems to lie behind the script which I am now about to quote. If it is accepted, Lorenzo's relationship with Saint Francis need no longer be regarded as something special and separated ; rather it will be seen as being a relationship inherent in every life and only requiring time to bring it into revelation.

With the wealth of affection peculiar to these writings, the script begins :

" Francesco is here, Lorenzo. I have come out of love for ye; I love ye, and have loved ye always. Ye are not only my brother, *fratro mio*, ye are also the beloved *figlio mio*, my son.

" My son in the spirit you understand. I feel to ye as to one who understands me, to whom I need hardly speak in words, so deep is the sympathy between us."

I was very moved by these words, but they had come so unexpectedly that my mind was hardly prepared to receive their full meaning. However, I asked Mrs. Dowden if the reference to Francesco being my father was merely an affectionate metaphor. Speaking for the communicator she said that it was no metaphor but represented a definite fact. Apparently spiritual parents were a reality.

By the next appointment, on March 4th, I had had time to give the matter a certain amount of thought. I asked at once if I might be told of spiritual relationships.

" Ye wish me to show ye," came the reply, " why I call ye son and also brother. Brother ye were to me the while we were in the Order. And ye were my most constant friend and companion ; but son were ye also to me, but that was before ye were my brother. And son in the spirit, not as of the body."

" When I became your spiritual son," I asked, " did

I partake of your spirit as a physical son would partake
of the bodies of his parents ? "

" Ye have partaken, ye are part of me, thy spirit is
part of mine. As the son to the father, so are ye to me.
And I have, because of this, been able to give ye a consciousness of my presence always. Since ye were a
child, I have been with ye."

" I take it," I said, "that a spiritual son is born on a
higher plane and descends to this ? "

" Yea, that is so ; ye are born in the spirit before ye
enter a body. Ye were born my son on the plane that is
sixth after this one. . . . The father's spirit hears all that
the son says to him and listens not for words only, but
for thoughts that are given as a daily offering to
Francesco."

" Do I come to your side in my sleep ? "

" Yea, nearly every night ye come to me and gradually
ye are drawn to higher planes. The spheres where ye
know without learning."

At this point I recollected having seen that a certain
John da San Lorenzo, who lived in the fourteenth
century, probably translated the Fioretti. If I had always
borne " Lorenzo " as a spiritual name then possibly
there was a relationship here. I asked if this were so.

" Now," came the answer, " ye have asked a question
that will puzzle ye, but at the same time, will please ye.
And ye shall understand this : This San Lorenzo is as
another and perhaps lesser father to ye. A fold of
Francesco is he, and ye are another fold. For the spirit
holdeth within itself other spirits, and ye are within
Lorenzo as ye are within Francesco, but nearer Francesco
than Lorenzo are ye."

If I hesitated to accept the name Leo, it was merely
that it made of me something, if not unique, at least

unusual. What I have just quoted may be the clue to a great generalization in which all are included.

Upon this point, a paragraph in *The Spiritual Universe*, by Oswald Murray, is instructive :

" All the Mighty Beings in these provinces " or very high planes, " have offspring passing through the several intermediate states " or planes, " of life . . . as well as on earth. The life current descends from our Angelic Parents, passing through their offspring in the intermediate states . . . till it reaches the outer earth." That is, we have parents on each plane. These are of increasing spiritual splendour in an ascending scale until the Great Father is reached. In a script by Hester Dowden of June 25th, the question of Spiritual Families was again taken up : " All that are born into this world," it said, " are born as belonging to a certain Spiritual Family, and these are the true relations that are given ye. When ye meet these ye know them, and the love that holdeth a Family together draweth ye into the circle and ye are at home."

A comparison was made between the various Families and the different colours of the spectrum, each Family holding its own quality or colour and being, as it were, a segment of the Divine Whiteness.

" I would that ye learnt a little more on this question of colour," said the script, " the colours of the Spiritual Families of man are of more than one shade. The colour that is ours is blue, a blue such as is in the sky on a summer's day, when the sun shineth. That is the blue of Saint Francis. But one colour also is there for each individual member of the Family. If ye could see the root of the Family and the folds that it holdeth in itself, ye would see all the shades that belong to that colour. Taken as a whole the colour is a deep one and hath a touch of rose in it which gave ye the colour in Hilborough Church. The colour as it poureth itself through the Spheres might touch on other colours, but blue would be in its foundation."

This is not the place to outline all the possibilities suggested by the communications, but the word " fold " is peculiarly of the Francesco of these scripts and is very illuminating on the essential unity of life behind apparently separated personalities. There is a script by Ethel Green, whose work will be discussed more fully later on, which seems appropriate here. It contains a phrase of similar meaning to Christ's : " I am the vine, ye are the branches," quoted a moment ago :

" Ye are the child of my spirit," says the script, " and have been nigh unto me from the Beginning and in no wise can ye be loosed from the spiritual link, for ye are as a blossom on my tree and can bloom on no other, for through me do ye derive from the Great Father of all and from that which is Francesco have ye been brought forth."

But the whole idea that each has a father not too infinitely above him and of similar spiritual and mental outlook is surely too simple and happy not to be true.

One catches a glimpse here of a divine domesticity, a shining Order, a Hierarchy which increases in splendour as we ascend, but which yet ends as a vital Family, a golden Household rather than as a Court.

XXVII

If Mrs. Dowden's script of February 20th was remarkable, it had a sequel which was quite as surprising.

I had friends, a Dr. and Mrs. Manning living in

Karachi, India, both of whom in different ways were psychic. I had not corresponded with either of them for about a year, but on March 14th I received a letter from Mrs. Manning describing a psychic experience which apparently was not merely impressive but which was overpowering. The whole essence of the experience was that she should write and tell me that Saint Francis of Assisi was one of my spiritual parents.

" Let calm and peace descend upon your soul. Even as you read this message the presence is with you of one who has ever attracted you to himself. Not a mythical saint, but a man even as yourself who lived and suffered among his kind.

" Through him you came ; Francis of Assisi gave you birth and inner life and he has kept watch and ward over you."

The whole message, of which I quote only a fragment, was written not only on the same day, but within an hour or two of Mrs. Dowden's hand writing : " Ye are also the beloved *Figlio mio*, my son."

And though afterwards, particularly in the scripts of Ethel Green, the idea of sonship was to be repeated and developed, never before had there been the slightest hint of this relationship until the hands of both Mrs. Dowden and Mrs. Manning wrote of it on the same day in different hemispheres.

XXVIII

Towards the end of March, 1932, the little church at Garstone which Francesco had called his Chapel of the

Fioretti was formally opened, and on April 22nd I was unexpectedly asked to take lunch with Alice Mortley. Until I arrived it had not occurred to me that these two occasions were in any way related.

At her request I had called an hour before lunch so that we could discuss various matters ; and in her direct way she began at once :

" Was your mind disturbed in any way when the Garstone Church was formally opened ? "

Alice Mortley's questions demand more than a conventional answer, and I hesitated because it was not altogether clear what it was she wanted to know.

" I mean," she went on, " were you perhaps angry at the time ? "

" I was, as a matter of fact," I said, " extremely angry with a lady who had introduced fabric which had upset the colour scheme of the church. The truth is that I find artistic insensibility difficult to bear."

" And you filled the little place with your anger while you were calling on the Holy Spirit to fill it with love ? . . . Don't bother ; we both know the answer. Listen : There is one, Brother Ambrose who has been helping Saint Francis with this, ' our church ' he calls it, and he is disturbed."

" What is the exact trouble ? " I asked.

" Ambrose spoke to me last night of the opening service. All was prepared, he said, for their church to receive its Chrism. But it still awaits it. There was some spiritual disturbance which prevented the work being fulfilled. Do you understand this ? "

" I understand perfectly up to a point, but I do not know how such things are dealt with."

" Are you away for Whit-Sunday ? And if you have arranged to be, will you cancel it ? "

" It is cancelled from this moment if that will help matters," I said.

" Whit-Sunday is by far the best possible day. You will go to the church if Ambrose wishes it ? "

" I certainly will, but at the moment I do not know what is expected of me."

" The work," she said, " is to consecrate that church, and Brother Ambrose has discussed the whole matter with me. You will understand that the real work is in higher hands. It is likely that Saint Francis will undertake it, but I shall be with you at the church and will bring two or three devout souls with me who will understand what is required.

" One other point, can you get to Garstone before you meet anyone ? It would be good to keep yourself and the day as something set apart until after the service."

" I can manage that quite well," I said. " You don't, I imagine, intend . . . well, to intrude upon the order of the service ? "

She laughed : " Anything but, my dear brother ; we shall be there for one purpose only and that is to support the act of worship in every conceivable way. You will, I think, find it wonderful. I feel that one day you will have great joy of all your churches."

Lunch was over before the conversation was ended. At length I arose to go.

" Good-bye, Brother," she said, " we will meet at the church. All of us who go with you must have one thought only : God's Holy Spirit pervades this church. We as persons do not exist."

" I understand."

" And about your own disturbance : We must bless this discordant element and feel the Holy Spirit within her."

It was like Alice Mortley to save that until the last. I make only one comment on it. In that one sentence lay the secret of Alice Mortley and indeed of all spiritual power.

" I will arrange that," I said.

" There must be no discord in her mind."

" You can leave it like that."

XXIX

Years ago I remember going to Glastonbury for the first time. I was driving alone at night from Bristol. The roads were unknown to me, my lamps were bad, and there was a mist.

The nearer I drew to the town the more thronged grew the air. All through the night after arriving I felt myself to be in the heart of a company of Brothers. And always there was that sense of light of which I have spoken before, light reflected from gold.

This memory came vividly back to me as I drew near to Garstone early on Whit-Sunday morning. For the air, like that of Glastonbury, was crowded with those who had splendid business there. The similarity of the two experiences was too striking not to be realised. This sense of the imagination being controlled from outside of oneself is not so common with me that it passes without leaving its impression.

Having provided myself with a key I let myself into the little church quite early. To one's outer ears the building was still and silent in the early mists. To one's inner ears the walls echoed the faint tumult of preparation, and there was no doubt as to its being the centre of spiritual activity.

Someone had put blue and gold flowers in every window and bright tulips on the small altar.

But I was soon by the sea again, watching its quiet breathing beneath the perfect blue ; and, I remember, there were two or three dolphins playing in the bay. The day was already warm, and moths danced among the grasses on the cliff. In my pocket was a copy of *The Little Flowers*. This book, by simple virtue of being there, has always given me a sense of presence and protection. I had no great desire to read, but was content to sit in the grass and watch the water below dimple and flash in the sun and to feel that invisible companionship which I knew to be about me.

Affection, moving and delicate like a fragrance, was borne on the very air. Blest, intimate hour of little things ! Its moments, clean and washed, were like points of dew.

xxx

It was now five or six minutes before eleven o'clock, and I made my way to the church. Within, were Alice Mortley and four friends. No word of any kind was spoken. I took a chair which had been kept for me.

The church gradually filled with worshippers, and the ervice began. As it was Whit-Sunday the whole arrangement was amazingly appropriate, and was in each prayer and cadence, a call to the Spirit. About the time of the third hymn the sense of spiritual immanence grew more profound. But it was just before the address that something quite definite happened. The hush had become almost tangible, when there was a sense as of fulfilment, as of a work being completed. There was Presence in the church.

We were all agreed afterwards about the moment. For me there was again that dull gold light, and then, quite vitally, the great Brother was in the aisle by my left shoulder.

At this moment he was not merely the little friend of the birds. Once or twice recently he had appeared to Mrs. O'Connell and to others, and he had come as a very great Being. In that manner he stood in the church, and the radiance from him streamed far beyond its roof and walls. In that same moment I seemed to know that about him were great angels; great of stature and of profound beauty.

Alice Mortley told me afterwards that at this time there was a descent of fire, and that I am quite content to accept. "Everyone in the church," she said, "at that moment received a blessing, and a blessing sufficient for his own needs. Even the restless children were caught up in it."

There was so very much more than I have written. I am so made that I perceive little more than the fringe of spiritual and psychic happenings, but here I had an unmistakable sense of perceiving on different levels within myself, and, as Francesco has put it, of "knowing without learning."

"All is in order, Brother," said Alice Mortley later. "The stone has been well and truly laid, the Power will remain when the building is gone."

It was just as her friends were about to drive her away that I introduced her to the lady whose sense of colour was not all that it may yet be; but who had, without in the least knowing it, opened a great door not only for herself but for all of us.

To realise Beauty is worth nearly every effort we are able to make. It is one of the few methods open to us of incarnating spirit within matter. It is the artists who make the dry rod to blossom, it is they who are gradually lifting earth heavenwards.

But still there are moments when I can bless the altar embroideries of Garstone !

To create Beauty is to stand for a little while on what is very nearly the last step of the spiritual ladder known to our world ; but Saint Francis, in whom Beauty lived content, represents to me the one step which lies beyond.

" When we were at Garstone," I said to Mrs. Dowden at the sitting which followed, " I had one or two very vivid perceptions. There were certain things I seemed to know."

" Yea," said Francesco, " ye were lifted out of the body for a moment, and as a child is lifted, that he may see over a wall that is too high for him, so were ye lifted and saw for a few moments that which is too high for ye."

XXXI

The first time I heard the word Glastonbury was when I was a child. My father told me on returning from a few days' absence that he had been there. Now I cannot tell which was the greater, my disappointment at finding that mechanical means could take one to this town, so occult and withheld, or my delight in having the domestic use of a man who had actually been there.

I cannot altogether account for the glamour, which for me even then clung to the name, unless indeed it was that some ancient memory was stirred. And this I am inclined to believe. My own view is that in all probability the Arthurian works of Malory and Tennyson gain much of their atmosphere for many of us from memories brought over from the past. I will confess, too, that certain places, people, books, and periods affect me in this same way. Annecy does, Glastonbury, Assisi, and St. Bernard's Hospice ; and among books, the John Alleyne Glastonbury scripts, all the ancient Franciscan works and particularly *Le Morte d'Arthur*, especially the Grail section, between which and *The Little Flowers of Saint Francis*, there is, to my mind, some sort of relation. Nor is this merely their romantic traditions, for numberless equally romantic and equally beautiful places leave me unmoved in the particular way I am considering now. Glastonbury, even in summer, with its laden charabancs, its red villas, and its tragical lack of great architecture, holds a wonder as though miracle, awaiting its moment, hung invisible in the air. Westminster Abbey, St. Peter's in Rome, even Florence where the poets, eternally young, still live ; all these do not for me create this same sense of spiritual dawn.

XXXII

It was nearly twenty years ago that I took my first journey to Glastonbury, but even now I cannot prepare to drive there without a feeling of launching out into unimaginable romance.

The charm is curiously immediate ; it appears to consist in a direct contact between Glastonbury and myself ; something which exists and is fully operative even when my mind is busy on other and external matters. As though it met me secretly in spiritual realms.

I have heard men say that they could tell blindfold when they were in a church where the sacrament was reserved. Without discussing that particular point,

Glastonbury creates in my mind a similar recognition as though Mass were being eternally celebrated there.

For some reason I have always associated Francis with Glastonbury, though why, I am not quite certain. Historically it is very doubtful if he, as Francis, ever visited England, though I and others have had scattered psychic evidence of him being both at Glastonbury and further north at Rockingham. This evidence, however, has not been sufficiently supported for me to give entire credence to it.

The first psychic mention of Glastonbury to me was by " John Alleyne " or Captain Bartlett, who wrote the scripts by which Mr. Bligh Bond discovered the various lost chapels and other details connected with the Abbey. He insisted that I had lived a monastic life there. This I found easy to imagine, and a belief which can remain vigorously alive, as this has done for fifteen years, becomes in itself a kind of evidence. My view being that in an active life the false intuition withers long before that. However difficult it may be to prove, my belief is that there is such a thing as inner awareness.

XXXIII

The earliest detailed psychic reference to Glastonbury, so far as this book is concerned, was in Mrs. Dowden's first script of January 30th, 1932, where mention was made of my architectural guides as having been at Glaston and Winchester : " These artists and workers," said the script, " were monks who devoted their whole lives to the thought of beautiful churches rising high into the air to the glory of God. Three of these have helped him, I, Petrus, am one, but there were two others besides. Johannes, not the one who is presiding here (Mrs. Dowden's usual control) but another who lived later, and one more who shall be called Jacobus."

Petrus here appears to have been speaking, and later the script continued : " Your Johannes is not the one who controls here, yours is the gentle brother who loved to write sweet words. Petrus will speak for himself : Petrus was the one that came to Glaston in the old days of the Round Church when the brethren were few and the people around mocked us. You and he were together at Glastonbury, if you will look back at the first message you got here, you will see that he speaks of that life."

The interesting point here, at the moment, is that Petrus and I were together at the time of the Round Church, which was, of course, the Wattle Church built by Joseph of Arimathea.

While speaking of Petrus, let me step aside for a moment from discussing Glastonbury to say that once or twice the scripts were held up for a little while by affectionate and indeed almost domestic greetings.

One instance was connected with Petrus, who only looked in now and then, and who is apparently, as a Guide, being put to a good deal of trouble on my account.

Hester Dowden's script of July 2nd, 1932, begins in this way : " Francesco is here, my brother, and before we speak, I would plead that the good Petrus should be permitted to speak a few words to ye. He is a fold and so are ye, and he serveth us both faithfully and well."

" Please," I said, " may I say to Petrus that I am ashamed of myself. He has been badly ignored, but he is very welcome."

" My brother," said Petrus, " I am not vexed with ye, for I know the sweetness of the Father and that all is

forgotten when he is near, but I would greet ye and tell
ye that I keep record on my plane of what the dear Father
tells ye, and that it is to be woven into a wonderful
pattern before the last word is spoken."

"Thank you."

"I have been much with ye, and in your company
I find great peace and happiness. I would not rob ye
of any of the precious moments that are given ye by the
Father. Therefore I give ye good greeting and bid ye
prepare yourself, for the pattern is not yet woven full;
more is to come."

"I am glad you are with me sometimes, Petrus.
Thank you for all you do. Whatever the Father weaves
will give me great happiness."

In the few moments of silence which followed there
was what seemed like a salute, no more than a friendly
movement of the dusk, and then Francesco continued. . . .

XXXIV

I have a script of June 3rd, 1932, which I would like
very much to accept, but so far, I have no corroboration
from other mediums. It makes a picture of Francis in
an early incarnation as a builder-priest at Glastonbury.
Johannes, Hester Dowden's control, is addressing himself to the sitter Ethel Green, of whom I shall have more
to say shortly :

"He" (Francis) "was there in the time of Patrick,
as he said." (It is supposed that I was with him at that
time.) "His incarnations in the Christian era came
rapidly one after the other, the space between was
comparatively short.

"Francis was considerably younger than King Ina, and

he was the priest who celebrated the first Mass in the Church of Ina. . . . Ina had the church built and dedicated it to the Holy Cup, though of this there is no record now. Francis was, as I said, the first priest who celebrated Mass in the Church, and he was also a builder, and almost what would now be called an architect. He had a hand in the building of the Church. Thus you see the connection with Lorenzo."

I am sceptical of all unusual communications which emanate from one medium only. If two mediums give a similar message, then at once there is ground for investigation. In the instance which I am about to note six mediums have been concerned.

There are two ladies known to me whose intuitions are untrained, but which I have known to be surprisingly accurate. One is Mary Hatfield whose letter about the name " Leo " through the Chinese control I have already quoted, the other is Mrs. Forrest whom I have mentioned also in connection with the name of Leo. For a considerable time during the development of the subject of this book these ladies, while known to me, were unknown to each other. Each had impressions regarding incarnations supposed to have been lived by me at Glastonbury, but, about 1933, Mary Hatfield was vividly impressed with the idea that Saint Francis in an earlier incarnation had been Joseph of Arimathea, and that he also had been my guardian at that time. Had it ended there the idea would probably have died unnoted. But more was to follow.

XXXV

Lucio, the control of Miss Francis, never failed to recognise those among her sitters who were in any way connected with me. Four such incidents occurred and the letter I am about to quote is a fair instance of this curious fact. At that time I was unknown to Miss Francis by name. Those who received this recognition were all most careful and reliable people who met Miss Francis at the British College and who could be trusted not to supply information to the medium. Indeed, in each case, the recognition came as a distinct surprise.

Such a recognition occurred at a sitting from the account of which I am about to quote. I received it in May, 1935, when abroad. What follows is taken from Miss Hatfield's own very careful notes made at the time. It is interesting as touching upon one or two points which are dealt with in this book.

For those unacquainted with Franciscan history, it may be better if I explain that St. Clare was the head of the feminine—usually called the Second—Order of Saint Francis. This community lived in the Convent of Saint Damian which stands just outside the walls of Assisi.

" The time was ripe," began the control, " for you to come, my child ; you are one of us, you are of the Company of Saint Francis. And you know Lorenzo. Of course, you know Lorenzo."

" Did I know him before I came to earth this time ? "

" Of course, you knew Lorenzo ; my dear child, you can remember better than that ! And you loved Clare."

" Was I with Clare on earth ? "

" You were with Clare in the convent at Assisi. You loved and worked with her. There was nothing you would not have done for her."

" Have I been on earth between the time at Assisi and now ? "

" No, you did not come again. Lorenzo has been on

earth between those times.   He was in a monastery at
Annecy and I was there, too, at the same time."

" Can you give me the name of the monastery ? "

" Yes, L'Abbaye Royale de Talloires, Annecy."

" Will you incarnate again ? "

" We shall *all* incarnate again and at Glastonbury.
Lorenzo will one day be given work to do there."

" When was Lorenzo there ? "

" Lorenzo was one of the early brethren.   It is hard
for me to remember it all.   When I come into this body
for a time it is harder for me to remember things and tell
them to you, everything seems heavy and dark.   Clare
was there, too, at that time, and Saint Francis.   He was
the leader, the head of the little company.   Yes, yes, yes,
I remember, his name was Joseph.   Lorenzo, too, had
the same name, and was one of the twelve with Joseph."

The sitting was considerably longer than my quotation
suggests, but I am endeavouring to delete all matter
extraneous to the purpose of this book.   It should be
said, however, that the details of this sitting, together
with others, were very fully stated once more by Helen
Hughes when Miss Hatfield again anonymously sat with
her about three years later.

Whatever view the reader may eventually decide to
take regarding the statements with which this book deals,
one point especially demands consideration, and that is
the repetition of the main ideas through different and
altogether disconnected sources.

XXXVI

At that time, although she lived quite apart from those
whose names appear in this book, my friend Mrs. Forrest,

in 1933, developed, entirely without suggestion from external sources, the idea of the Saint Joseph incarnation.

Nothing further happened until July 16th, 1936, when I had a sitting with Mrs. Grace Cooke. Ten days later I had my first sitting with Helen Hughes. Neither of these mediums had ever seen me before, nor had they any normal knowledge of me. In both sittings the main occasions dealt with in this book were instantly given; at once, too, the controls of each gave out the idea that Joseph of Arimathea had been my guardian and instructor through many lives.

None could have listened to either sitting without being impressed by the singular ease with which the mediums spoke, showing almost domestic familiarity with Franciscan history, and with the general tone of seriousness and almost of solemnity with which many of the statements were made.

There was a remarkable sitting at the British College on April 22nd, 1937, with Eileen Garrett. Uvani, her control, had discussed me as one who had an ecclesiastical mind and who designed many churches. He also described my method of design, which was interesting.

There had been silence for a little time when, in a way startling to me, he said two syllables which were unintelligible but which sounded like " Yo-seff." I repeated these several times to try and arrive at understanding, when he said :

" He prepared you for initiations for service. He says you were a Brother. He means you were a Brother of an Order. Yo-seff of Arimie."

" Ah ! " I said, becoming intelligent again, " please continue. Was he then a Master ? "

" Master . . . Master ? Yes, if you must use such words. ' But,' he says, ' call me Father, Brother, not

Master. I loved you as a father loves a son. I worked with you as a brother.' . . . He says you have been with him right through. He loved the birds in the garden and they gathered about him, and he caused the white rose to bloom. And then there were the little furry things. . . . Their footsteps did not hurry away from him. ' Tell my son and brother,' he says, ' that all life is one, all is God.' "

" This is very interesting, Uvani," I said. " Does he go very far back in my history ? "

" He goes all the way back with you, and there are many, many lives. He says : ' Together, my son and I have looked for the place where Apollonius was buried, we have worshipped in the temple, we have fed in the little market-square, we have sought each other in the chapels on the hills, in the woods and thickets, we have prayed to God in the little city ! ' "

" Which city ? "

" In Assisi."

" Oh ! . . . But was Joseph of Arimathea in Assisi ? "

" He says," went on Uvani, " that his name was then Franchees, Franchessa . . . something like that."

" Francesco, perhaps."

" Francesco ! Yes, yes, Francesco, that was the name he said."

" Uvani," I said, " all this is very good."

" He says you have a statue of him as he was then."

No comment of any kind was made by me which could suggest one word of what I have written here.·

I will not press this idea further ; let it speak for itself. I can only say that I am bound to it by some living thread that is heavy with affection. There is no ground trodden by Joseph which is not beautiful to me.

XXXVII

With regard to the statement made a little while ago that I had lived a monastic life at the Abbaye de Talloires, this had been given to me before. Indeed, in my first sitting with Miss Francis, the control told me he had known me there. His name, he said, was then Caesaro Peronne.

Being near the Rhône Valley in 1935 when I received Miss Hatfield's account, I took the little mountain railway which runs on its perilous ledge from Martigny to Chamonix. Spending the night at Chamonix I went on next day to Annecy and eventually, among the hills around the lake, found the Abbaye de Talloires. As it is now a very charming hotel I stayed there. The cells, practically untouched, form the bedrooms. It was May and hot. I remember on a blue, still morning taking coffee and rolls by a very beautiful well in the cloister garth. But the memory which will always remain impressed on my mind is that of the almost overpowering smell of incense which greeted me as I was shown into my bedroom on arrival.

When I sat next at the British College the control of Miss Francis reminded me of this. He claimed it as a manifestation of their own to welcome me into my old cell.

XXXVIII

" Thy memories shall awaken," said Francesco in an early Hester Dowden script. " Yes, but as fragments, as precious jewels that flash for a moment. Ye shall, however, have more and more of these."

And this has proved true ; they come, to use his own

words, "as birds that fly up into the air and vanish again." Memories of the far past generally rise to consciousness when their emergence will be of help to the toiling soul. The dark remembrance is balanced with the bright to guard against undue strain. Over-exaltation being quite as harmful as despondency. They appear as consequences of previously forgotten acts and are clearly intended as warnings or encouragement. They appear when the pilgrim will be strengthened by knowledge of them and when the purpose of life is becoming clear to the ascending soul, and its ideals are reaching definition. At first they are often mistaken for imagination.

"Light shall fall upon the dark places of thy memory," says a script of Ethel Green, "and the pictures shall flash forth from thy former lives ; all the phantom show shall pass before thine eyes, and ye shall see the shadows bearing the germ of that which ye shall become when life hath shaped ye to the spiritual man.

"As ye see thy past, so shall ye have assurance as to thy future, for ye shall perceive the foundations of the building and the design of the Supreme Artist which it is for ye to carry out, fulfilling the vision which He giveth of Beauty and Perfection."

Another script through the same hand again makes clear the purpose of recovered memories :

"We who have guided ye to this decisive point now make ourselves apparent and our will clear. Daily ye shall find that the mists melt from thy mind and the clouds from thy path, and that the purpose of thy being taketh form.

"Images shape in thy mind, figments of the past and shadows of the future. Soon shall ye see the rounded whole and understand the love that hath led ye and fashioned ye, and that now offereth ye the choice of celestial bliss and complete surrender, or a further cycle of wandering."

I had a curious confirmation of these things, too complex to give in detail, but which refers to a time when I forgot the Brethren, left the protection of Talloires, and indeed left Europe altogether. The script of the Brethren, received on the day of the Holy Cross, from which I shall quote shortly, marked the end of a separation which began before this present life. Their words brought healing to a consciousness which is buried deeper than the casual memories of normal experience.

The confirmation came first during 1938 through a chance conversation I had with Marjorie Livingston, who is so well known for her occult work. Mrs. Livingston gave me a vivid picture of the life after the break, portions of which I had already seen. Indeed, at one point I interrupted her to complete what she was about to tell me, as I am sure she very well remembers. This confirmation was again supported by a proxy sitting I had with Miss Francis early in 1939.

It would be stepping aside from the main idea of this book to give the details of this separation, but it will serve a useful purpose if what I have said suggests that progress is by no means inevitable, and is often far from being continuous, as that word is ordinarily understood.

The conversation I had with Marjorie Livingston suggested to me the possibility that memories brought over from past lives may be more frequent than is usually recognised.

When I was a child I had a recurring dream which was terrible in detail and intensity. It would not be too much to say that about the first seven years of my life were overshadowed by it. For a day or two after the dream

I would go about with a sense of horror upon me. Until the age of fourteen or fifteen I would go to considerable trouble to avoid anything which might remind me of it.

Mrs. Livingston asked me if I had any memory of the infliction of torture. Instantly the old and almost-forgotten dream came to my remembrance. I asked her to describe what was in her mind; this she did, telling me where the trouble fitted into a past life. And, behold, my dream was before me.

XXXIX

It was Mrs. Forrest who, towards the end of 1932, first saw Saint Clare and recognised her essential relationship with the Brethren. In the first sitting I had with Miss Francis, in April, 1934, Saint Clare was mentioned as one intimately associated with the Order as it is now. She was also seen vividly in an aura of blue and gold by Miss Francis in the lucid first moments of waking from trance. Saint Clare, too, came into the Geraldine Cummins script of November, 1936.

Since then, through Mrs. O'Connell and many others, and especially through Mrs. Helen Hughes, she has entered, as one might say, into the daily life of quite a number of people, especially of those whose intuitions are beginning to awaken.

Just as she came to Mary Hatfield, she came also very strongly to Mrs. Burnham who grew to have a great personal regard for her. Indeed, Saint Clare brought a peculiar loveliness into the lives of many of her friends. I shall not attempt to deal fully with this in this book, but one curious incident should be told.

The little group of rooms, rather like a bungalow, where

I do my work, has its own garden, and Mrs. Burnham, who had followed, as they occurred, many of the events contained in these pages, wished to make an offering to Saint Francis. By June, 1934, she had already planted a rose and other flowers for him, when it occurred to her that she could plant a lily as a special tribute to Saint Clare.

The seasons, however, go their own way and make no attempt to support enthusiasm. The year 1933 had developed a drought ; 1934 very nearly became a national tragedy. My small garden was so hot and dusty in July that a bush of wild fuchsia fell over owing to the complete lack of support in the dry, sandy soil. Saint Clare's lily was transplanted in early June. Its stalk was in bud at that time and was about twelve inches high.

Owing to my having an unusual amount of work I was unable to give the garden the attention it needed. In weather like a furnace the lily was left unnoticed. Towards the middle of August I chanced to walk by it and found the stalk and buds hard, brown, and shrivelled. I felt ashamed, I ought to have given thought to it.

On August 27th I ran up to London to carry through a great deal of business and to take, at the British College, a long pre-arranged sitting with Miss Francis. The sitting opened as follows :

" Well, Lorenzo, there you are ! "

" Well, Caesaro," I said, " here indeed I am. Did you know I was coming ? "

" Lorenzo ! did I not arrange it for you ? Of course I did. Now, how is the lily ? "

There was a chuckle at my astonishment.

" You thought it was dead, didn't you ? "

" Now, Caesaro, this is really rather good ! "

" No, no, it is easy. Do I not see it ? But it is not

dead. Clare is very interested in that lily, and watches over the lady who planted it. . . ."

The curious thing was that this proved to be true. The lily did still live, and, though there exist far better gardeners than I, it is green as I write.

XL

My sittings with Mrs. Dowden lasted through the greater part of 1932. Towards the middle of the year my anonymity was dropped and I became a friendly visitor at her house on the somewhat rare occasions when I found myself in London.

In August it was arranged that we should meet at Glastonbury, and eventually we did so on the 31st. With Mrs. Dowden was a friend, Mrs. Eleanor Newnham; she also had the gift of automatic writing, and, in connection with this, there was a rather unusual little incident.

The day was a hot and beautiful one, and we sat on a grassy bank listening to the soothing sounds of a distant lawn-mower, not far from the Chapel of Saint Mary which stands on the site of Saint Joseph's Wattle Church.

Mrs. Newnham sat on my left and Mrs. Dowden on my right. Both had writing-pads, and presently Mrs. Newnham's hand began to write. Two seconds after, the lawn-mower, which was a large mechanical one, was driven rapidly by us and close enough to startle Mrs. Newnham. Her hand stopped, and at that moment Mrs. Dowden's hand began to move.

The writing was as follows, Mrs. Newnham ending at the word "mortal"; "My son, there is betwixt us a bond which is greater and stronger than all those which bind the ordinary mortal. . . . It is a closer bond than ye have any knowledge of now as ye are ; for it is the merging and blending of one soul into the other soul, out of which a new manifestation in the flesh is shown." I have always regarded this instant continuation of an interrupted message through a second writer as being one of the most remarkable minor evidences for external control that I have myself received.

Miss Mortley, who had no knowledge whatever of this Glastonbury visit and with whom I had had no communication for some months, wrote to me a few days after, outlining the idea contained in this last writing. The letter is before me, but is so personal that I hesitate to quote from it directly, but it suggests a recent closer bond with Saint Francis as of auras blending. One sentence, underlined, reads : " You are in the aura of Saint Francis now."

Those who know their own natures will understand me when I say that these ideas, and similar ones in this book, have been vital enough to cause me to bend and break much of my life which did not march with them.

Mrs. Dowden wrote very considerably during this summer's day and there was much conversation. One point, I remember, interested me particularly, and that was her inability to explain why the scripts of this book and other ecclesiastical writings should have come through her. She had, she said, leanings to the Arthurian legends, but no ecclesiastical instincts whatever. " Wherever these writings come from," to use her own words, " they certainly are not from my own mind." I should associate her myself far more with the Greek outlook than with mediæval romance whether of Francis or of Arthur.

A section of her script of this day may be of interest. It is, of course, not evidential, but it carries the charm of all the scripts which bear the name of Francesco.

" This is the greeting that Francesco giveth to his son and brother, and the two that are near to him and do act as his mouthpiece. All that is, is God. . . . When ye come to the Holy Place, pray that ye shall be given understanding of the glory and the greatness of God. And pray more earnestly that ye shall be given humility and the willingness to learn. For in humility and with hands outstretched to God, ye shall reach Him. And in all that comes down to ye from Him, from the Archangels to the smallest of the insects shall ye see the Lord that made ye.

" Now will I tell ye that I have much to say that is connected with thyself in this Holy Place. For as ye came I heard ye say that here and there ye have felt the sanctity that surroundeth us here, and that is but natural, for here ye are at home.

" The vale that ye speak of, the vale that is called Avalon, hath an inner and deep meaning in it. It can be called the Holy Ground as well as the earth upon which this Abbey standeth. Ye, Lorenzo, who art own brother and son to me must feel the call that this place maketh to ye.

" This brought ye here to-day, and whenever ye are in sorrow, yea, when ye are sick, ye will find this place will heal and comfort ye in spirit.

" When ye were here ye were not a lay brother as ye suppose. I would that all who follow me should be humble, but ye were at all times one that used the mind and spirit, and great in the counsels of the Holy House were ye in your day. . . ."

XLI

Mrs. Dowden and Mrs. Newnham had decided to spend September in the south, and on the 12th, a boisterous day, I found them seated in an incompletely sheltered spot on the high hills above Studland, overlooking a great landscape which included Poole Harbour and its islands.

This occasion is impressed on my mind because here, impromptu, was written what proved to be one of the last of Hester Dowden's scripts belonging to the series included in this book. I will quote its opening words for their charm :

"Lorenzo, beloved brother, this place seems full of winds that do quarrel and strive with each other, so that it is difficult to speak.

"Here, to-day, I wish to tell thee that the day at Glaston was a blessed day, that Francesco hath a greater power since then, that he hath made a closer approach to thee and that thy father hath his arms more surely around thee. This may give thee comfort and help thee. . ."

Unknown to me a great change was about to take place in these communications, a new writer and a greater gravity were to enter.

THE SECOND BOOK

XLII

ON my return home on the night of October 24th, 1932, after a short absence, I found a small package awaiting me. The lady who had left it had left also a verbal message that she would like to call and discuss the contents with me. My mind was probably preoccupied with other matters for I forgot to open the package until some time during the next day. When I did take off the cover, several written pages disclosed themselves, of which the following was the first to be read :

" This message to my son is to cheer him and to give him faith that much more is to come from me to him. For in truth he is but at the beginning of what will prove to be an experience that has seldom occurred before.

" Francesco hath so far spoken but in fragments, and he hath scattered these fragments among many persons. This is to convince Lorenzo. It cometh not through one alone, but through many channels.

" Here in this house in which I write I find peace. I sit here in a fair green field and the birds come around me to speak to me. I warn my brother to beware of houses that are not as a fair green field, but as a hedge of thorns that will prick away his faith from him. For as a sound hath it gone forth that Francis hath come again, and as in the time that is past there have been many false prophets, so many will claim to have been with Francis. Lorenzo will know me by the language in which I write, which he hath from three or four persons.

" I send him my love and my blessing and I promise

him that whatever work he may lay his hand to, it will prosper."

To say that I was amazed to receive this script is to speak moderately. I found then a note among the papers. This made it clear that the package had been left by a lady whom, for a few moments, I had met about six months before at a friend's house. I could not pretend to know her, but I had spoken to her. On looking through the papers I was most deeply moved by their purport and by their beauty.

The lady who signed herself Ethel Green and who lived in Ireland, I came to know well. During the day I was able to see her and she explained the circumstances around the message.

It appeared that six months before she had had sittings with Mrs. Dowden. These, of course, were unknown to me. Johannes, Mrs. Dowden's control, had asked her to allow him to write through her hand. He begged her to follow his instructions: "Sit passive," he said, "and when you have sat with eyes closed for about five minutes, then take your pencil and try to write. I should like," he continued, "to include you in the Francesco communications if I can. This case is a case of psychic weaving. All the connections Lorenzo makes with people who are interested in the subject are significant in some way and are there to add to the evidence he already has.'"

XLIII

Mrs. Green had made a few halting attempts to write, but eventually returned to Ireland, not too successful, and contented herself with meditation.

During the latter half of October, 1932, however, she was back again in England with Mrs. Dowden and had three sittings, on the 19th, 20th, and 21st. Francesco appeared and occupied the whole time.

Portions of the scripts which were given were then written by Mrs. Dowden in the usual way, and portions were written by Mrs. Green who held the pencil, Mrs. Dowden's hand resting on hers.

This method, however, did not appeal to Mrs. Green, she preferred her hand to be perfectly free. Eventually Mrs. Dowden put her hand on Mrs. Green's shoulder when at once, and very clearly, a voice spoke to her. Her hand moved with the voice and she wrote :

" My daughter, give me your hand and let me send a message to my son, for such he is. Tell him that Francesco desires him above all things to devote himself to that Greater Life which is around him, above him, and below."

That was the first script written by Ethel Green entirely alone. I have many times watched Mrs. Dowden's hand write rapidly and unerringly when she was in the midst of a lively discussion on some quite unrelated subject. There was here a distinct difference between the mediumship of the two ladies, for Mrs. Green required complete silence. Her gift appears to be not so much automatic writing as clairaudience.

Writing to me a year later, she said that she should always consider her first hearing of the voice of Saint Francis to be the most blessed event of her life. As I write now, seven years after, I am certain that she would, with great joy, endorse her own words.

After this message she was told to call and see me in Hilborough and ask me to sit with her.

" Ye shall sit with Lorenzo and he shall touch ye with his hand. Power from Francesco shall pass into him and so will ye have the power of both Lorenzo and Francesco. And none shall hinder or prevent ye."

Various details she was bidden to arrange, and a few small instructions were given to her for me. " I beg my brother," was written, " when he sits with this daughter who hath written first to-day, to sit without speaking, and in silence will my voice be heard."

XLIV

This was the commencement of a series of one hundred and thirty scripts. They were written with few exceptions in Ireland and between October 25th, 1932, and March 12th, 1934. The great majority were sent at the rate of two a week. They were produced in periods of personal trouble and during illnesses and, if I may say so, they were even more bravely written amid the thousand distractions which beset every normal and reasonably unselfish life. Moreover, they were continued through a summer of almost overpowering heat.

I think I ought to say that the correspondence between Mrs. Green and myself was always slight and impersonal. I mention this because there were many times when there was a quite definite relationship between the script and the deeper movements of my mind. Our letters were not sufficient to account for this.

Ethel Green came over to England, I believe, twice for short holidays during the seventeen months in which the writings were produced. We naturally met, but from the beginning until now she has known practically nothing of my personal life. She has since written scripts unrelated to me. Those with which this book deals would contain about fifty thousand words.

In November, 1933, during one of her visits and at the end of a sitting, Mrs. Green pointed to a corner of the dark woodwork above the fire-place. In that spot, she said, had hung a star. This star, it appears, always comes into being during the communications. Ethel Green belongs to an old Quaker family and has that power of straightforward judgment, common sense in fact, combined with mysticism, which is almost the peculiar possession of the Society of Friends.

Probably there was a certain feeling of constraint when, on October 25th, she first sat in a strange house to wait on the spirit. I think, too, that she rather expected long detailed descriptions of previous incarnations. Glastonbury, I know, was in her mind. We had just before been discussing Mrs. Dowden's script describing Francis in the time of King Ina and had been baffled by the statement that Francis and Patrick had met, as Saint Patrick lived three hundred years before Ina. But, unexpectedly, we had found in a book of Bligh Bond's that a hermit of that name came to Glastonbury from Caerleon in the time of the Saxon King.

Both of us had our minds filled with questions about Glastonbury, but the Power behind the writing had other ideas.

After a halting script or two, there was one evening, November 5th, when the barriers were down, and, sitting silent beside her, I watched her hand race over the paper. When she stopped it was merely to rest an aching arm before beginning again.

There were altogether nine scripts written in this particular way before she left again for Ireland. They are too long and occasionally too intimate for complete inclusion here. There had been brief references to Francesco's life at Glastonbury, for we repeatedly pressed questions upon him about this, but these were ended by this paragraph :

" My life at Glaston was to me an experience whereby I became filled with the Holy Wine, for in that place of many memories came I closer to my Lord, and my soul was made strong for to bear the burden that all must carry when the Vision has pointed out the way."

XLV

I had, and probably by that time we both had a strong feeling that it was not now the details of the life at Glaston of which he wished to speak, but rather of the way to Vision, so gently did he lead us from the external to the vital.

" My son will be used," he wrote, " as a vessel to carry the Wine of the Spirit, even as I in the days of earth. For the time is at hand when he shall hear the call and strength will be given him. . . .

" Have no fear of the future, for at all times am I with ye, and great shall be thy joy as ye enter into unity with the Father.

" The call will come to ye in the day when thy cup is full, and when the power of the Holy Ones has been gathered from the four corners of the earth. . . .

" My love encircles and enfolds him, and in the darkness shall he see me, for much will I ask of him, yet the burden will be light for the Father will bear it with him. . . .

" My son, be not dismayed at the perils of the path, for thy Father who loveth thee hath trod the way before and knows the weakness of the flesh and the shrinking from suffering. . . .

" First of all must ye guard thy mind from all impurities such as trouble the natural man, and, secondly, ye will need to protect yourself from those who would rob ye of the faith that thy Father hath given thee. . . .

" Take heed and be watchful, for many will be thy temptations and the great ones of the earth will call unto thee, yet heed them not, for not to such will my words come in their fullness. And see that ye lose not the purity of the faith. In darkness and silence shall ye hear my voice, in the hush of the evening, and in the song of the bird. . . .

" I have much to say unto thee as to thy life. Look only to the inward light . . . and take no heed of such as would counsel thee for thy so-called good, for there is a wisdom which is folly and there is a foolishness which will lead to the Altar Steps of God . . . a humble heart will bring thee to where the angels abide. . . .

" The time will come when my son will reach out to the life that was mine, and many and sore will be his trials, for the flesh suffereth as the spirit ascendeth, and brave must be the heart that wills to climb the heights.

" The day cometh when ye will arise and become as I, an offering for humanity. For to those who are gifted with the Spirit all must be surrendered and nought with-held. For only according to the fullness of the sacrifice can the blessing come, and the Father asketh for such as can cast all aside even as did he. For these are the tools with whom will be remodelled the earth.

" The day cometh when ye shall see my face, for I will satisfy the desire of thine heart. And in that day shall ye be blessed among men.

" Rest now, for the time hath fled."

XLVI

I have quoted in no particular order, and almost at random from the nine scripts which were written with me.

I cannot read them without being deeply moved. There is a definite call in them and nothing could persuade me to make them public, but that some other will hear the same clarion and feel the same impulsion towards humility and a clearer air.

The idea in the last words quoted from Ethel Green's script was reflected four years later, that is to say, on November 14th, 1936, in the script by Geraldine Cummins. I had asked if one day I should see him.

" That," he replied, " will be given ye in a time when ye are not expecting me ; suddenly, clearly as that vision of the Seraph that was mine. And I shall appear when thy spirit needs me, as that ineffable Vision was mine when it was all my need. My blessing, Brother, remember the birds and me. Francesco di Bernardone."

The writing of many scripts is only made possible by the interaction of two minds. The process is not by any means fully understood, but the Glastonbury scripts are an instance, among many others, where the power only came fully when Bligh Bond and John Alleyne were together. I was troubled lest, when Ethel Green left for Ireland, the conditions might not be satisfactory. I therefore put the question to Francesco.

" Yea," he replied, " my daughter will write for her Father as she doth now, when the seas roll between ye. . . . My children, thy Father will care for ye and the work of my daughter shall not be impeded by distance, but rather shall she grow in strength."

When the two weeks closed which are represented by

these scripts, I felt as I think the Brethren must have felt when they descended the long slopes of Alvernia after the day of the Holy Cross.

Something had gone from them, something of marvel had come to them. Francis had been the whimsical, lovable Brother, the eloquent preacher, the centre of pretty miracle. But was there not new Power in him which was beyond the things of earth, which had a strange majesty and which could only be apprehended dimly?

To me Francis was still the " Little Father," picturesque even, but he had been revealed as having Royalty.

XLVII

One of the results of writing a book of this sort is that all manner of memories are evoked which otherwise might never have been recalled.

One such has just come to mind and is a great surprise to me. It will be remembered that 1928 was the year in which the name of Francis was first used in connection with me by a psychic. In 1924 I was staying in London with friends. My hostess was particularly busy over various social affairs and I was pressed into service. My duty was to convey some message to a lady whose name I forget. She lived near Baker Street.

I drove over during the morning and presently found myself chatting amiably in her drawing-room. I was just laughingly denying psychic gifts when the lady, who had no normal knowledge of me whatever, said: " Are you an architect, for I see you surrounded by dozens of houses?"

" That is exactly how I see myself," I replied. " I am buried under with them."

" Do you believe in reincarnation ? " she asked.

My beliefs on this subject were then very vague and a trifle antagonistic, and I said so.

" Well, whether you believe it or not, you have been a monk ; and a monk is greatly interested in you."

I can remember now how lightly I took this, bracketing it with the fortune-telling of church bazaars.

" You will not always design houses, you are to design public buildings ; though I cannot tell their purpose. But I can see," she said, " the people walking up steps to enter them. This monk who wears a short beard will help you in this work. He is a foreigner and a great soul ; Italian, I believe."

That is the whole of the memory, and at the time it had less value than the coffee I drank while listening.

Among the first nine scripts of Ethel Green, from which I have just quoted, occur these words :

" My son, great has been my joy to draw thus near unto thee, even as in the days of the flesh. For many years have I longed to draw near, but the time had not yet come to reveal what manner of life I had prepared for thee."

If my almost obliterated memory of 1924 is linked up with these words, written in 1932, there is a picture created of the unwearying patience of spiritual greatness. I think now that this gift of waiting, this devotion to those who are still indifferent and immature, shows us one of the most remarkable aspects of those whom we call High Beings.

One day we, too, shall acquire this gift, and it may be that it is not until then that we shall make any considerable contribution towards the unfolding of the universe.

XLVIII

In April, 1932, Alice Mortley told me that when she was considering the breakdown of the opening of Garstone Church, she saw in the night Francis as a Great Being ; his hand was on my shoulder, for I accompanied him.

" Who are you ? " she asked.

" One who stands beside the Brother," he replied. " One who has love without desire, and would give only the true help of the Spirit, and who would protect."

If a stranger were to glance over the records of the communications from Francis, I think that the one thing he would see before all others would be the beauty of the affection which they contain.

This is particularly noticeable in the scripts of Ethel Green. And as for some time I shall be quoting from her writings, perhaps it will be understood that all quotations are hers which carry no other acknowledgment.

There is a love which is like a nocturne, shadowy and deep, like music across a windless night. But the love of Francis is like a bright morning in the spring, very positive, very free and bright, full of fragrance and warm sunlight. It is, moreover, protective and gentle and makes no demands for himself.

I think few of us realise here, especially in this mechanical and chill age of frustration, what a splendour of generous love awaits us. It is no sombre affection of duty burdened with reproof, but a buoyant support, living, joyous, and abundant.

" My peace doth surround ye," says Francis, " and my love is as the wing of a bird over its little one. . . . My son, rest thyself in me and be at peace, for nought shall harm ye, neither shall ye be anxious as to the future, for thy way shall be made plain and angels shall guard ye as ye walk thereon ; and the joy of the Heavenly Hosts shall be thine. For ye are indeed blest in that one is thy companion who hath passed through the shadow of death and who bringeth to ye gifts of love and wisdom from a fairer world. . . ."

" My son, I abide in ye, and my heart beateth with thine, for ye are with me, and the Eternal Light sheddeth rays upon thy path. The love that is in thy Father shall never fail ye, but shall bear ye through the bitter and the sweet unto the perfect day."

In a letter of January 17th, 1933, Ethel Green wrote :

" When the power is good and Francis is able to get through his whole message, as it draws to an end I can feel him striving to convey to you in vital phrases the intensity of his love. It surges around me and I say : ' How shall this be put into words that he shall grasp even a little of what his Father would send ? But there is no sufficient language to express his thought.' "

" My beloved son," he says himself, " little can I tell ye of my love which hath borne ye hitherto, and will encompass ye to the end. For the language of earth cannot image forth the tenderness I bear ye."

It is no exaggeration to say that this book could be filled with such passages.

" My son, my love calleth to ye night and day, saying ye are joined unto thy Father and are upheld by his spirit. He will carry ye on his wings to the high mountains, and show ye the glory of the Lord."

There are no claims in the love of Francis. Whatever there may be of instruction there is no trace of domination. His love sings free of all desire and is on every page and is implicit in every word.

XLIX

Perhaps the warning should be given that this book
leads on to no splendid and final achievement, for I
who write have arrived at no halting-place. To those
who cannot yet call themselves Masters of Compassion,
but who, like myself, are still of the common Brotherhood
of Humanity, I can say that if they will, they can receive
much help from the gentle and sane directions contained
in these scripts. They have caused me to make great
moral effort, but never have they caused nervous tension
or intellectual strain. These pages have been written
by one who merely, though quite definitely, has turned
his face toward the Path. More than that it is impossible
to say, for I am conscious that to some of the apparently
most simple questions I have no answer unless it is the
answer of Francesco :

"Love conquers all, and is the only weapon that ye
need. In the power of love did I live, and love hath
brought me to ye and hath made us twain one ; and
love will be thy guiding star until the perils of life are
past."

Other than that I know little which will help to solve
what are known as intellectual problems.

From the standpoint of these scripts, knowledge is of
secondary importance, even as it was to Francis on
earth. The keynotes are the ancient ones of Love,
Sacrifice, The Cross, Poverty, and Humility. "Ye
shall give thine all, and thyself also. For ye shall be a
brother to the needy and the oppressed. By the love
which is manifested through ye will the heart be touched.
But only as ye love can ye minister, and to love, ye must
see thy brother as he is—like unto thyself."

Francis always was simple at heart. Great outlines of

cosmic organisation were never his merchandise. Reincarnation is always here taken as a matter of course, but the speech which dwells upon Initiations and the Brotherhoods of Masters is not his. Karma is recognised : " Earth," he says, " hath given ye much, but ye must pay thy debts before ye can enter among the Blessed." Much which is usually called esoteric knowledge is tacitly accepted, but is never pressed home as being of prime importance.

The Brotherhood of Francis as outlined here is not necessarily the only power in the spiritual realms. It represents one movement in a great universe, a development within a family rather than a cosmic organisation, notable just as his own Order and life here were outstanding. But, like the work of a great artist, it tends to ignore bookish standards and to burgeon in response to some central force. His instructions, one imagines, are precisely such as he had discovered true for himself. " Not by words shall ye preach," he says, " but by thy way of life, by the offering of self, by the light with which I shall endow ye, which shall show to all men that ye are indeed my son, and that thy Father doth manifest himself in thee.

" For the world hath need of much, but what it chiefly lacketh are those who will be as Christs to their generation, those who will show by their lives that there is naught which cannot be overcome by faith and to whom the invisible hath been revealed in glory. For in these there is Power which can redeem and re-create the souls of men ; the life which giveth life and which cometh from Him our Master and our Lord ; to Whom all honour and praise.

" For in Him will ye work, and from Him do I come that many souls may be gathered unto Him."

There may be other paths than that outlined by the Francis of the scripts, where knowledge, definite, accumulated scientific observation, is of the first importance. Of such things I have no sure information. I have instead, doubts ; for, so far, intellect, placed before that affection which is Brotherhood, has led the world to catastrophe. The achievement of knowledge for personal enlargement seems never to have occurred to Francis. "This is my desire for ye," he says, "that ye shall strive even as did I in my earthly pilgrimage ; that ye shall give all, lose all, and being empty of self shall be filled with Light which is the soul of the Divine. This shall ye bring to such as sit in darkness and in the shadow of death."

It is seldom gain to which he refers, he desires no preferment for his followers ; never does he urge the accumulation of power and the gathering of prestige. "My will is that ye live as one called to serve and to obey. . . . My son, I will guide ye step by step as my power groweth within ye. For I shall take all from ye, and ye will come to me as one newly born, loosed from earthly shackles and rejoicing in the freedom of thy Father's home."

L

The mind of Francis was never far from vision, and we may be sure that no single note of the starry music of Christmas was lost to him. It was Francis who turned the cave at Greccio into a stable and, amid the cattle, celebrated Mass and laid the Elements in the straw of the manger. For him the Child was born anew each Christmas Day.

On Christmas Eve, 1932, I had just returned from a visit to Assisi, of which I shall have more to say shortly for it was singularly beautiful, when I had a long script from Ethel Green.

" Say to him," says Francesco, " that I would speak to-night of the coming of Christ to earth. For the time draws near when many will be celebrating His birth, and ye among them. Much joy did thy Father take with his beloved companions in greeting the Christ-Child, and many times did ye enter into the rapture of his soul, when after the night of darkness and of prayer came the glory of the dawn and the Saviour as a little Child was in our midst. For in those days great was the Light around us and we lived illumined by His presence. So great was the power that naught came between our souls and Him, and the trials of earth were borne, as it were, by another body, but we dwelt in the secret places of the Most High. My son, I would that ye should realise that at these times of joy does the Christ indeed draw near in majesty and glory, and the earth is lit with His splendour. We, His servants, who have entered into His undying love, gather around Him with great triumph, and salute Him who is the Lord of High Heaven and the Eternal Child born anew in the heart of man."

LI

There is no doubt that from about this time changes began to take place within myself. There must, I feel, be many in these troublous days who are being prepared for spiritual service. If what follows gives them a sense of companionship in their personal difficulties I shall be glad, for the difficulties created by the fact of such preparation can be severe and of necessity must be faced alone. That it is some part of a universal process

which at some point in a long succession of lives takes
place in each individual soul, I have no doubt. After the
paragraph just quoted, the script continues :

" As the Christ draws near to His loved ones, even so
do I draw nigh to ye ; and this Christmastide will I
envelop and enfold ye so that ye shall know the fullness
of thy Father's love, and in his abundance shall ye be
nourished and renewed. And I will pour into ye my
life force so that no more shall ye faint and be weary."

Had these words stood alone there would not have
been considerable impress left on me. But, three days
later, Ethel Green received the following : " Francesco
speaketh : Say to my son that it is my will that he be
ready to receive me, for I am fully come and I will
envelop him. For I, his Father, will inhabit him and he
shall dwell with me. And truly will I lead him by the
straight and narrow way. . . . With me shall he pass
through the abyss, and with me shall he rise to where the
Morning Star shineth and praiseth God."

To keep the mind of the various mediums free and
uninfluenced it was agreed by all who were known to
each other that no communication should be made
between them concerning any of these writings.

As none of them ever appeared guilty of curiosity this
has not been difficult. It is sufficient now to say that
Hester Dowden had, and still has, no knowledge of the
trend of those of Ethel Green's scripts from which I have
just quoted.

LII

On January 9th, 1933, I had been asked by a friend,
not connected in any way with these writings, to join
her in a sitting with Hester Dowden. The idea being

that I might " supply power." It is open to question if this end was achieved. But what did happen was that during a discussion upon archæological excavations Francesco stepped in and gave consideration to a point which had recently been occupying my mind :

" Ye will not eat meat after a time when the body needeth it not, because the spirit will be in thee," he said, " I will explain this to ye, Lorenzo mio. The body must take what it needeth while the spirit is entering in, but once it has entered the body, the body mattereth not, but the spirit fills it and feeds it also. Ye are drinking in the spirit at the present time, so ye need the body still and ye must not fast or abstain from what buildeth up the strength of the body."

Mrs. Dowden confessed that she knew less than I as to what was meant by the spirit entering. The matter did not end here, but continued to occupy some place in seventeen scripts for a period extending to a little over six months. Two of these scripts were through the hand of Hester Dowden and the rest through the hand of Ethel Green.

" For many days," was written, " have I poured forth my love upon ye and now ye know wherefore I have approached ye. But ye have yet to learn the work which I would have ye do. This shall be revealed to ye as ye are able to bear it, for naught will there be to gratify the natural man in the way which I shall lead ye. Others shall walk with ye upon the path, and by my light and by my path shall they bring their offerings to the feet of Christ. . . .

" Now that my spirit doth abide in ye must ye take cognisance of all that ye know of the life of thy Father on earth. Much there is that will be a guide unto ye in divers difficulties. . . . For naught now shall be small to ye, but in all things must ye keep watch and guard lest the enemy pierce thine armour.

"The upward path is one of constant care, and though the angels guard thee thereon, yet thine own effort can never slacken, nor can ye pause to look back. . . .

"Only for a season will thy mind remain darkened; the day cometh when the light shall break through and ye shall see with the eyes of the spirit."

LIII

Early in May, 1933, and during June, another note appeared in these communications. Ethel Green's script of May 8th contained these words:

"My son, I would give ye my instructions as to thy life. Ye are now at a point when I can show ye the next step which must be taken without delay." And then as though speaking to Ethel Green herself: "My child, ye shall hear me again on this matter and ye shall give the message to my son. He will receive from other sources the same instructions and will understand that I desire him to obey. . . . He hath been faithful to me and I will give him power to obey even as I demand his obedience. This period of unfoldment through which ye are passing," the scripts continued, "hath in it much of difficulty . . . it is the effort to throw off the grasp of Mother Earth who hath nurtured ye for so long and to be born of a fairer Mother, even she who beareth the stars in her bosom.

"In the death pangs of the natural life we are filled with the transports of the life supernal, and the measure of our joy is the measure of our pain. For the world hath no place where he who leaveth it can lay his head. The foxes and the birds have their place of refuge, but the re-born child wandereth alone, ministered unto by angels in alien lands.

"My son, the final struggle is a bitter one and pierceth to the bones and marrow; for all that a man is must be taken from him before he can put on the garment of the Holy Ones and wait upon his Lord."

If there is a Francis whose gentleness reminds us of Bethlehem, and whose tenderness wins all wild things, there is a Francis who knows and accepts Golgotha.

It was now that Alice Mortley, knowing normally nothing whatever of my life, wrote the note I have already quoted: "This is your Everest, keep your vows."

Ethel Green's scripts continued: "My son, I will speak to ye of thy life, for I have brought ye to a place where ye shall pass over a bridge and find thyself in another sphere, and from henceforth the spiritual man in ye shall rule. . . . Thy work requireth a dedication of both mind and body.

"Ye have come to a place where there are two paths; the one will lead ye to earthly greatness, and the other to a narrow way where all is desolate and full of sorrow. For this is where ye walk alone through the valley of the shadow. . . .

"Ye have obeyed me in all things, and it is my will that ye go forth as a pilgrim carrying the Cross, the sign of thy faith and thy condition. For the Cross signifieth the abandonment of earth life, and showeth that ye are born into a higher world where ye are transformed by the spirit and delivered from the power of the body. Therefore, having received thy freedom, ye are called to the children of the captivity; they who groan and seek for release from sorrow, yet who comprehend not that they themselves have forged their chains, and that only their own hands can break them. . . .

" My life floweth through ye, and ye are at one with thy Father. Therefore do I test ye that ye may know the weak joints in thine armour and strengthen them against the day of battle ; for now is the time when ye make ready thy weapons and perfect thyself in all knightly exercises, for ye fight an unknown and treacherous foe who riseth up against thee when ye are not aware ; who sleepeth not, but waiteth always to strike and to destroy.

" As ye seek to rise, the Powers of Darkness will gather around ye, for the light ye show is to them a challenge to mortal combat, and they will pursue ye while earth calls ye her child, and the body bears ye within its frame. Therefore, my son, know thine own weakness, and that the walls of thy city are exposed to hostile attack, and seek help from Him who seeth the secrets of the heart and understandeth the temptation of the soul, to whom all things are visible and who walketh with ye in the Darkness as in the Light.

" Listen for the voice within, and lay hold on my staff of power, and I will be a guide to thy feet and bring ye at eventide to thy Father's House. . . ."

LIV

No purpose would be served in detailing the events to which these communications refer. It is sufficient to say that the one who produced the writings had no knowledge of them. A wide sea and a space of three or four hundred miles separated the hand which wrote the scripts from the man to whom, and about whom, they were being written, yet a precision unerring and almost terrible marks their progress.

" The hour before the dawn," Francesco continues, " is ever the darkest, and little will it avail if ye fight thy battle before the foe appear. For now do ye waste strength and thought in imaginary combats, not yet knowing what manner of trial ye will be called to face.

" My son, a veil is drawn over the future which I may not lift lest ye be distracted from thy task of preparation ; for what will frighten a child will but raise the heart of a man, and a man ye shall be before we give ye a man's work. . . . Live in the present, yet with the knowledge that to-morrow shall bring a greater revelation, and that thy burden will be fitted to thy growth, and strength shall be given when the Holy Ones call ye forth.

" My son," he continues, " ye have need of thy Father, for thine heart is sore and many are thy trials. Yet would I bring ye consolation and respite, and wrap ye in my love that sheltereth ye from the harsh world.

" Ye shall be given joy from grief and strength from sorrow and thy darkness shall be turned to light. For even as ye mourn, thy tears are wiped away, and the Blessed One raiseth ye to the place of His abiding. Have faith and fear not, for short and bitter are the days of earth. Learn ye thy lesson while ye may, and seek to accomplish that for which ye were brought forth, lest we give thy talent to another and ye be left to grieve for thy lost endeavour. . . . Therefore do I dwell with ye and tend ye and nourish ye with the life of the Vine. But as in the natural world there are times of darkness and of light, so is it in the soul of man. The light given for a space is withdrawn lest the growth be too rapid and . . ."

Whatever the cause may have been, the scripts ceased abruptly here, that is to say on July 4th, 1933. The period

from May 1st until July 31st was to me one of great
darkness. There was in it a quality of dread which I
cannot bring myself to discuss. It was unremitting and
all but intolerable during each of the ninety-two days of
these three months. That this affected the production
of the scripts I feel certain.

Ethel Green was in Ireland; my few letters carried
no indication whatever of my life, but her scripts followed
the profound movements which were taking place
within. When her writing ended abruptly in the middle
of a sentence she wrote telling me that the last paragraph
of her script had been strongly impressed on her mind,
and in the days which followed this sentence was repeated
to her again and again: " The darkness is the gift
of love as truly as the light."

LV

There was complete silence until August 1st when my
desolation ended abruptly, and, without any warning
whatever, or any communication from me, the writing
in Ireland began again. The winter was ended and the
words of Francis came once more like spring weather.

" My child," he said, " I am with ye, and I bring
consolation for my son who hath been through deep
waters. Hear me, for I will speak. My son ye have
suffered much, for thy way hath been hard for ye, and
veils of darkness have enwrapped thy soul. Ye have
lost much which was precious unto ye, and that which
ye have gained is not yet apparent. Look unto Him
who leadeth ye in green pastures and by still waters and
who bringeth ye to the secret place of the Innermost. . . .

" My beloved son, these many dark days have I

desired to speak unto ye and to comfort ye in thine afflictions. For in the outward life ye have suffered sore, and in the inward places of thy soul hath been darkness, and thy Father hath seemed hidden from thy sight.

"This is the trial of which I have warned ye, that ye should pass through deep waters; yet shall they not overwhelm ye, for the Hidden Arm is around ye, and at no time have ye been forsaken.

"When the light shineth once more for ye, my son, ye shall see thy gains and rejoice in thy victory. For the new dawn will excel in beauty aught that thine eyes have rested upon, and ye shall find that thine earth-garment hath been refined as with fire and the dross purged away. Ye shall look back and understand that thine agony hath brought ye to a height that ye could attain in no other way, and thy tears shall be as sacred drops which sanctified and cleansed thine inward parts.

"My son, we, thy Protectors and Teachers, see life not as dost thou, for to us naught is of value save the growth of the soul, the gradual deliverance from the illusions of earth. And to us it is a time of rejoicing when the test can at last be given and the beloved one raised a step nearer the abode of the Blessed.

"Though we grieve with the suffering one, yet our vision embraceth that which is and that which is to be; and, in the gladness of the coming day, the dark night seemeth but a shadow through which we guide our well-beloved children. Therefore, my son, gaze ye ever on thy goal, and know that thy life on earth is given ye that ye may gather strength. For our Lord needeth those that are mighty men of valour, whose hearts quail not during the tumult, who have overcome the flesh and the desires thereof, and whose armour hath been forged and perfected by fire and by labour. For by endurance shall ye triumph, and the steadfast man shall climb to the stars.

" Be assured that I am with ye ; and as thy feet crossed the deep river, my hand upheld ye. My love hath been thy shield and the Powers of Darkness shall not prevail, for ye are sealed unto the Lord, and thy work is before ye.

" The peace of Christ be with ye, my son, for ye shall enter into His rest. Thy father, Francesco."

LVI

Before I leave this phase I would say that, like most spiritual movements, the crisis through which I had passed had an outer aspect in which others were involved.

My friend, Mrs. Forrest, was often given good counsel. If I had an impulse to call I usually found that I had acted with unconscious wisdom.

I ought to say that practically the whole of her knowledge of Saint Francis was gained through vision. I believe that, until early in 1939, she had never read anything whatsoever about him, and such things as had been discussed between us were the outcome of seeing a few of Ethel Green's scripts and of her own clairvoyance. This I looked upon as an advantage, and took good care never to discuss with her any material point of Saint Francis's life so that her vision might remain quite uninfluenced.

In the middle of my dark three months I chanced to see her. At once she told me that she had seen " The Master " (this was her own name for him). " He was with a large dog," she said, " and the dog was behaving very affectionately towards him. I was told to give you this message ; that you shall win the man who troubles you as he had won over this dog."

" And he used the word ' dog ' ? " I asked.

" No, I do not think he did, he was pointing to it."

It became quite evident after careful questioning that Mrs. Forrest had never heard of Francis winning over the ravenous wolf. This vision, which was remarkably apt, impressed me greatly. The reader is, of course, entitled to his theory of submerged memory, but Mrs. Forrest has a simple and direct mind, and a month after, when I told her casually of Saint Francis and the wolf of Gubbio, it was immediately apparent that her vision had for the first time become completely intelligible to her.

LVII

Life became increasingly beautiful as the clouds of the dark three months passed away. There would be an occasional note from Alice Mortley : " The way to the Highest will now be much more direct. . . . During sleep you rejoin the Group ; the old paths are there and lead into the Sacred Way of Eternal Love and Service."

Two apparently small things began to emerge. The word " Group " occurred in the scripts with greater frequency, and inner awareness became clearer and more sure of itself.

Echoes of the dark months occurred now and then in the writings of the next few weeks : " I bid ye be of good cheer, for ye have passed thy test, and now cometh the time when ye shall receive the fruits of thy travail. . . . Remember that the way is hard and there is no easy victory. . . . My son, rest in me and be at peace, for I lead ye. I have shown ye the hidden path and have revealed the Secret Glory of the Unbegotten. Ye have come to the moment when the spirit gathereth strength. . . . Knowledge shall be given ye as ye grow in power ; and as ye serve thy brethren, even so will the angels guard ye and make ye a channel for their gifts to the children of men. . . .

" Tender hath been my care for ye, though the darkness hid me from ye. . . . Those who are to be as cupbearers to the Blessed One must give up all and be purified as by fire. Much suffering must they pass through, yet each trial is a step to a higher state of being, bringing joy to the soul. . . .

" Ye have heard the call : ' Arise and come,' and the way hath been made smooth for ye, for that is thy Father's care ; for he wills not that ye shall suffer save in outward seeming. For in that must ye be an ensample to such as shall gather unto ye. But in the inward parts shall ye find harmony and peace and the light of deathless love that hath linked ye through the ages till this day of thine awakening. In the silence of thy soul shall ye realise my presence and accept the gift I offer of Life which transcends thine own and which awaiteth the hour to declare itself.

" Speak to me from thy heart and I will answer in thy dreams and in thoughts which I will give as ye need help. For much dost thou ponder, but the day will come when ye shall see clearly, and the mists of dawn will have passed away."

LVIII

September 14th is the " feast of the most Holy Cross." . . . " On that same morn," says the writer of the Fioretti,

" he saw descend from Heaven a Seraph with six wings resplendent." This, of course, was the culmination of the forty days' fast of Saint Francis on Alvernia. Although almost devoid of any gift for recalling anniversaries, it is seldom that this day passes without my being aware of its special meaning.

On the anniversary of 1933 I woke early, conscious from the first that this was a day of marvel. The very morning seemed golden with the glow of " Alvernia all aflame," and it was a few moments after waking that I received the script which I am about to set down here :

" My son, hear my words, for I would that ye become grounded in the faith and in the knowledge that love hath lifted ye and formed ye, that in the time to come ye may repay the gift, offering all that is thine upon the altar of Humanity."

At this point the script seemed to break and to begin anew :

" We, thy Brothers from the Hidden Realms, look upon ye, remembering the experiences of lives shared on earth, when we strove and stumbled, yet still triumphed in the holy name of our Lord ; when the shadows of earth fell across our highest endeavours, and we comforted one another when all seemed lost save faith. So now do we return to our Brother in the land of his captivity, understanding all that he suffers, and offering him the love that was his of old, opening for him the door of the world of wonder which lies beyond his ken, showing him the golden glory wherein we dwell.

" We who served the Father and followed him to the death, yea, and beyond the portals of death, to the high Mountain of the Saints, call on ye to enter once again into our company. And when the light burns dim and the outward world is hushed, to listen for the music of our

voices and join with thy comrades in their offerings of
praise.

" Our Father, the blessed Francis, hath permitted that
we send ye these few words, for he desireth that ye
become as one of the Spirit Band, though separated by
the veil of matter, and that ye realise the closeness of the
tie which hath ever been between ye and us, thy companions of the past and thy fellow-workers in the
Harvest of the Lord."

That, to me is utter beauty. I have to confess that
I have few possessions which I treasure more than this
script.

LIX

Five days after came the following :

" Ye have received the message from thy Brothers in
the Inner Spheres, and thine heart hath been lifted up
in joy that the veil hath in part been raised, and the
threads of thy past lives revealed. For the present is but
the outcome of that past, and in the dark womb of Time
lieth the future, waiting to be unravelled. Ye tread the
one Path, but there are many stages, for it stretcheth
from the Limitless Beginning to the Infinite End, yet
is the thread never lost, but it weaveth the pattern
prepared by the Eternal Father ; and those who entered
conscious life with ye are linked in all stages and at all
times, whether dwelling in matter or in the Inner World.

" And now thy Brothers of the Spheres are gathering
to ye, for ye are the one chosen to enter the human
body and endure the trials of mortal man.

" Many years have ye wandered, seeking for ye know
not what, and thy Brethren have waited by thy side
until the time when ye should be delivered from the

bondage of the flesh, and the spirit within ye rise to the heights from which ye came. Now is the time of thy return and thine awakening, and great is their joy that ye have conquered the temptations of the outward world and have purified thyself in thine inward parts, that the veil is thin between ye and them, and that they can speak to ye words of cheer and greet ye once again after the storm and stress of earth.

"For the years of darkness are past, and from henceforth ye shall be shown thy Path and will be conscious of the light around ye and the task to which ye are appointed. No longer will ye be treated as a child from whom we ask obedience, but we will reveal the laws of Destiny and the Heavenly Wisdom which guideth the children of the Spirit.

"My son, regret nothing in the past, all experiences have been necessary for thy growth; they are as garments which ye have outgrown. But now that ye have come to the time of flowering see that ye bear thy blossoms in full and perfect beauty, letting no stain of earth pollute them or canker touch their heart, but offering the fragrance of thy being to the Pure Heavens to which ye aspire.

"My love is with ye, and thy Brothers clasp thee by the hand, blessing ye even as do I. Francesco."

LX

It is possible that the following slightly adapted quotation from *The Voice of Isis*, by H. A. and F. N. Curtiss will help towards a better understanding of the phase of three months with which the previous pages have dealt.

" The experiences met with at this period will consist
of events which will force him (the Neophyte) to face
himself, and bring to his consciousness every secret and
open fault ; events which will force him to gaze into the
eyes of the self he has created . . . which contains
the essence of the desires, ambitions, passions, and
aspirations of his personality. It is the Dweller on the
Threshold that each must meet, recognise as his own
creation and conquer.

" There can be no dodging the issue or turning back
from these events, for it is a mathematical law that he
cannot pass on until he has acquired strength to conquer
these faults one by one as they are presented to him. If
he refuses, or is unable to conquer, his soul must wait
and work . . . until it grows stronger, and until another
cyclic opportunity for advance is afforded.

" It is not a matter of pledges or words." . . .

That quotation seems to me to be exactly correct ; but
the shock accompanying these experiences can be so
profound that it must be met to be understood. It
breaks completely the idea, so strongly entrenched in the
most sincere of us, that one can pay reverence to a
Teacher and yet disregard his teachings. Worship is
not enough. . . .

LXI

The words " Family " and " Group " recur many
times in all the communications upon which this book is
based.

The word " Family " would seem to comprise all who
belong to Saint Francis whether consciously to themselves
or unconsciously.

A Group is a company within a Family, and the word is used in two senses. First, of the Group to which we actually belong; this may be mainly on the Inner Planes. Secondly, it is used of the Group which is gathering, or which will eventually gather, about us and to which we owe assistance. This assistance is far from being a careless or passing charity, for in the ultimate we shall find that our only way to achievement is to take the Group with us.

Those who in the Spiritual Realms are gathered about Saint Francis are referred to in various ways; the Brethren, the Spiritual Group, the Heavenly Counterpart, or the Heavenly Band.

" Ye have effected a closer link with the Heavenly Counterpart," is said in a script of Ethel Green's, " and from henceforth will receive the vibrations of the Group without difficulty by withdrawing from thine outward life and opening thy soul to the influences which enfold ye."

And again, in a script two months later, " Thy work shall be in unison with the Heavenly Band . . . as ye are knit to them by ties of old."

These references are to those who dwell in the Spiritual Realms, but the most frequent references are to those here on earth.

" Many there are," the scripts continue, " who seek the hidden wisdom. . . . These shall be gathered together, and the springs of the Celestial Life shall be opened to them and they shall see . . . the fruits of the Spirit and the vision of a fairer world. Be ye wise and heed not the spoken word, listen rather to the motions of the soul and join thyself only to those in whom is the print of the nails and the Passion of our Lord. For only with such will ye find peace, and only with the Little

Children of Humility will be founded the new Order which we desire to see created on the earth. . . .

" Many shall greet ye in my name, and seek to lay upon ye the commands of men and outward forms of faith even as they sought to bind me in my days on earth.

" But ye shall escape from all such, and in the silence of thine heart shall ye find the revelation of the work which we lay upon ye ; for the trodden path shall be to ye a snare, and thy spirit must soar beyond the forms of life familiar to thine age, to a conception yet unborn, but which awaiteth the realisation and adoption of the children of grace.

" For the Seer must precede the builder, and the vision foreshadoweth the accomplished work ; wherefore have we drawn ye unto us that ye may perceive in spirit and translate into mortal language that which man shall achieve as the Breath of Heaven bloweth upon his brow.

" For life is to be raised to a degree where spirit forces will operate in a manner new and incomprehensible to this generation, but for those who are found ready and whose lamps are burning will come the call : ' Behold the Bridegroom cometh, enter ye in.'

" A great flood of illumination is to be poured forth upon the earth, and need is there for vessels who will hold this Light and transmute it to the needs of the weaker brethren ; for well ye know that through human minds we pass the principles of the Infinite Spirit who dwelleth in us, His children, and reacheth out through us to the uttermost bounds of His Kingdom. For on the upward march none can be left behind, but all are alike precious, and reflect according to their kind the glory of the Creator from whose great Heart they issued forth, and to whom they return bearing with them the jewels won in many a hard-fought battle, and wearing the Crown of Life and the bright and Morning Star.

" Thy work will be given ye as ye grow in grace, and will be the natural outcome of the reality of thine experience, so that at no time shall ye say : ' I go forth to serve,' but always : ' My life is my service.' Even so shall ye give of thyself in love and humility."

LXII

Many of the scripts which refer to Groups on earth are unfortunately so interwoven with personal matter that I feel unable to reproduce them here ; and those which follow I have felt obliged to abbreviate.

" Ye are more and more in my way and in my beliefs, and around ye I am drawing those that can help ye and that ye can help. Ye must not go from the world without giving that which was given ye to those that ask for it. Ye are part of me, and these others are of the Family but not so close." So ran Hester Dowden's script. Those which follow are again from the writings of Ethel Green.

" Many are the days which must elapse before thy Band will be prepared to face the foe . . . the Group on earth must be united with the Heavenly Counterpart, and then will it be possible to utilise to the full the energy which is now being stored."

This script was one of the few by Ethel Green written in my presence. I was able, therefore, to put a question as to what constituted the Heavenly Counterpart.

" My son," came the reply, " ye shall hear even as ye desire, for many are with me who have served as I during many ages, and their strength is added to my own, and we seek to establish a Group which will respond to our inspiration, and they shall be receptive of the Heavenly message."

Answering another question the script continued :

" Many of my children are called, but the time hath not yet come when ye shall rejoice in their presence ; they will be prepared in secret . . . and will be brought to ye when ye have need of them, and in the day of thine adversity.

" For these who come are the children of the Father, and they have heard my voice within their souls calling them unto myself, yet knew not whence the voice came nor whither it would lead them. And they shall rejoice as lost children who have found their home, and whose wanderings are ended. They shall find the peace for which they sought."

And again : " I will gather my servants from the four corners of the earth, and there shall flow between them the sustaining flood of mutual love and common purpose so that they shall move forward like an army of the spirit world.

" Soundless upon winged feet they shall lift the heavy burden of earthly sorrow and the shadow cast by sin, and purge away with the fire of their consecration the legacies of the past."

In another script of this same period, that is, the spring of 1933, an outlook wider than the Franciscan Order is given.

" Others of my brethren will manifest also through their children, for we are not alone in this work, but already the air is vibrating with the presence of the Holy Ones who have been gathered together and are concentrating all their forces on this generation. Ye shall meet with such of these children as are harmonious

with my Ray. For these will co-operate with us as the
work progresseth. For the children of the Holy Ones
are spread abroad through many lands, and each hath his
work prepared for him, and his way of approach."

"Only as ye become immersed in the Immortal can
ye understand the meaning of thine existence ; and only
as ye understand thyself can ye enter into the lives of thy
fellows, for ye are all of one nature, children of the same
Father with the same needs and like destiny. Therefore
seek in all things to obey the voice within, and listen not
to the world's music, for within thy soul is the Song of
Dawn and the murmur of strains infinite and remote,
the chords of the universe resounding through the living
heart of God."

In connection with these discussions on Groups
there were often prophecies. These, however, were
sometimes of a kind which I have felt it wiser not to
emphasise. I will let a script by Ethel Green of January
6th, 1933, be representative of them.

"Ye shall learn the nature of the Group which it is
my will to form. For in this present age much hath been
forgotten of Ancient Truth, and I desire that ye shall
share with such as love me the simple life of the early
days when man lived nearer to God and to nature, and
had not lost himself in the struggle for gain.

"In the New Age that is upon ye life will swing back
to what ye call primitive conditions, and much of what
has well-nigh destroyed the life of the spirit will cease
to exist."

LXIII

Just as the word " Group " was used more frequently
as the scripts developed, so it has become more generally

frequent of recent years in occult literature ; and Groups, whether these be entirely of the visible world, or of the visible world with spiritual ties, or entirely of the spiritual realms, are an essential part of spiritual development.

It has been interesting to me to find the idea of Groups, as suggested in these scripts, developed in *The Road to Immortality*, by Geraldine Cummins, though in Miss Cummins's book they are viewed from a slightly different angle. This book is compiled from automatic writings apparently coming from Frederic Myers.

Whether the members of these Groups have a definite " blood " relationship comparable with our earthly idea of families, or whether they are congregations of similarly disposed spirits, and merely that, is not disclosed. I personally incline to an essential " blood " relationship.

Myers does not write as a final authority on these matters, and indeed who could ? He writes rather as an explorer in realms strange to him who puts down impressions of recent discoveries. This means that revision and adjustment are almost bound to occur with him later on. But there are quite a number of suggestions which are useful.

He insists on the vitality and reality of the Group. It is not merely a gathering together of detached human beings. There is, whether inherent or acquired, a living, and, one might say, organic connection between its members. At some point in their evolution the members have the use of each other's experience ; access, as it were, to each other's minds and memories.

Myers gives it out that many of the memories which certain people claim to have of past lives are in reality experiences of their brothers filtering into their consciousness. They are, in fact, tapping the Group mind.

He makes a point that reincarnation is not nearly so

drastic, in the sense of being repeated over and over thousands of times, as one might imagine. Each member having organic connection with all other units of his Group, the experiences of those passing through an earth life are communicated to each individual of the company. That is to say the efforts of the member on earth chemically affect each member of the Group, whether any particular member is on earth at the moment or whether he is, as we say, in the spirit. In other words, his sufferings cleanse his brothers. Indeed his earth life is not so much for the discharging of his personal karma as for discharging the karma of his brothers. He has come to earth on behalf of his Group, and, using the language of the Church, he has taken upon himself their sins. This is a form and a very vital form, of the Christian idea of bearing one another's burdens.

The more one discovers of spiritual organisations the clearer does it become that the foundation, the very profoundest supporting principle is not the gathering of knowledge, not the accumulating of saintly power, but it is sacrifice ; the sacrifice by a loving heart, gladly given. Not self-help but service is the key of heaven. "If ye lift thyself ye perish," says one of the Francis scripts. "As ye minister so shall ye be ministered unto."

LXIV

In passing, genius may have some relation to the gradual awakening of a soul to conscious relation with his Group. The genius has added the value of his brother's experiences to his own. Speaking electrically, the battery has been increased from one cell to many.

We are wont to regard reincarnation, if we accept the

idea at all, as being one of so many cast-iron laws imposed by some Supreme Authority, and bearing with equal weight on each individual in the Cosmos.

Is it conceivable that souls can, to a certain extent, organise their own education and evolution? "It is always a question of desire when the soul returns to earth," said Johannes, Mrs. Dowden's control. "It is always a matter of subconscious choice; it may, however," he went on, "be almost a compelling choice."

Now whatever faults Western peoples may have, they have at least the rudiment of an idea of Brotherhood. The Western man can better create organisations than the Eastern. Team-work is understood here in a way unknown in the East. The Eastern mystic, or saint, lives in a sort of isolated grandeur, an asceticism of solitariness. It is conceivable that he might enter into incarnation thousands of times without mixing mentally or spiritually with any other single being.

Did our Leaders discover a way out through Brotherhood, whereby we all bore the sins of the whole Family and pooled results? Was this Christ's great revelation which the East with all its accumulated wisdom has still failed to grasp? Is the Group idea particularly Christ's?

It is possible that the old troubled subject of the Atonement may be seen more clearly if we regard the whole world as Christ's Group. It is possible that His life and death made a Family of those who would, through which His power could flow : "Life is within ye which is in touch with the Greater Life," say the scripts. As a phrase, "the Blood of Christ" is symbolic, or it remains unexplained. But if we can accept what I have called an "organic" connection between members of a Group, as I personally do, and as the Francis scripts do, then we have a basis for understanding the Atonement. For the life-force, or "blood," flowing freely through all, any outstanding degree of spirituality of one would benefit each member of the Group. Incidentally the Leader could not achieve freedom until the whole Group had attained.

We have here a clear view of our own future when in turn we ourselves shall become the Leaders of our own Group. We, being of Christ's family, are permitted to carry on His knightly tradition of succour. Here, also, is shown to us that we are allowed to bear with Him the weight of the Cross and, entering into the living fellowship of our Spiritual Brethren, are filled with their strength, and by this power awaken in the souls of those weaker and immature the fire and gold of the Grail.

THE THIRD BOOK

LXV

I T is doubtful if any one town and any one man were
ever so bound together as Assisi and Saint Francis.
In some remarkable way they express one another. And
though Saint Francis was spiritually far from being small
as his city is small, yet affectionately we regard him as
little, and he loved so to regard himself. Indeed all with
which he was associated was " little " to him, including
his birthplace. In the scripts of this book, he referred to
it generally as " The Little Town." He himself is, of
course, known the world over as " The Little Poor Man."

In one of Mrs. Dowden's scripts, written not for me,
but in my presence on November 30th, 1932, and dealing
with matters unconnected with this book, the word
" Francesco " was unexpectedly written and was followed
by : " Go ye to the Little Town," and a few moments
later : " I beg that if ye can, ye visit the Town that is
mine."

Actually, at the time, I was passing through London
on my way to Milan, and though there were reasons
why I should return quickly there was an affectionate
brushing aside of these. " When ye return," continued the script, " ye will write out all that happened in
Assisi. Ye shall keep a record of all this, and it will
afterwards be found to be the beginning of an interesting
history."

That was seven years ago, but I did go, and kept notes
of my stay. Although I had been before, and have been
several times since, I always look upon that particular
visit as having a beauty and an intimate charm of its

own. In the words of a script of Hester Dowden's, written on my return : " Each day that ye were in the town sat we together for a time, and this communion hath drawn us closer together. It was well that ye made the journey. Ye have seen with your own eyes the place where Francesco lived and worked and worshipped, and ye have stayed long enough to take into yourself some of the memories that are there."

That, indeed, was the atmosphere I felt from the moment I was welcomed into Assisi. And Assisi does of itself offer a welcome. The very air stirs with life, and one is met continually by the past, not dead, but living and affectionate.

LXVI

The day following my return, that is on December 17th, I went over to Chelsea, and, without any preliminary conversation other than a greeting, the script from which I have just quoted was commenced. This script cannot in the strictest sense be called evidential, but it certainly shows the clearest knowledge of my movements in Assisi.

As was often the case with previous scripts, this was written at an almost incredible speed and during conversation.

The writing would not be intelligible without some outline of the life of Saint Francis and some note on the general appearance of Assisi. I will, therefore, set down a few of the characteristic details of both.

There is one curious fact connected with this visit. Ethel Green was at this time writing regularly two scripts a week. Having left England hurriedly I had not the opportunity of letting her know that I was visiting Italy. As the train ran along through the starlit snow on the Loetschberg ledge, high above the Rhône Valley, I had the first vivid sense, indescribable as music, of meeting the Brethren. Let me halt a moment to say that this sudden view of Switzerland, this particular aspect which opens incredibly after the dark tunnels beyond Kandersteg, has become completely associated in my mind with Saint Francis and the Brethren. Visp lies two thousand feet or so below, the torrent which rushes through it to the Rhône one knows to have been born of the glaciers of the hidden Matterhorn and the great peaks of Monte Rosa. The white remote mountains of the Simplon, veiled against the stars, lie ahead, and here in this noble beauty, on the very edge of Italy does the welcome of the Brethren begin. They were indeed in that air which rang over the ice of those high levels. The gay, completely understanding affection of Francis and of the Brethren filled all space.

At that moment Ethel Green in Ireland commenced a script which ended abruptly, nor would any other word come to her until, having left Assisi, I was passing back over that same path across the Alps.

The first script, written as I was about to enter Italy, was touched with that whimsical raillery that won so many hearts :

" I would speak to my son," it said, " and this would I say unto him : Remember the words I spake to ye when we were together in the flesh, how that I chid ye when ye obeyed not, but answered with words which I had not given ye. Even so do ye remain obstinate to-day, speaking of thy Father as of one enshrined in the heart of the world, though verily he be as ye."

The reference is to the episode described in Chapter

Nine of *The Little Flowers* when Francis wished Leo to condemn him, but Leo would only bless.

The script by Ethel Green, written eleven days later as I sped once more over the Swiss snows on my return, began : " Francis has come again to write through his daughter and to send his benediction.

" These many days have I been with my son in the place of my birth and I have shown him much of myself which he knew not before. Gradually do I unveil my face, that he be not blinded by my glory, and I clad me in my grey garments which he knoweth well, and verily my son doth realise that once again are we united by the love which dwells in his heart for me.

" For this is the magic by which he has called me to himself, the key to all the mysteries of life, for without love there could be no creation, nor any light or beauty brought to the earth."

LXVII

It is difficult to know whether the spiritual atmosphere of Assisi is that of a cathedral or of a friend. At any point one will meet the breath of incense, which I personally find beautiful, but there is also a simplicity, a protectiveness, like the feeling of one's home in childhood.

A coronal of hills between three and four thousand feet high surrounds the plain of Spoleto in Umbria, and it is at the foot of one of these, Mount Subasio, that Assisi stands. The town is walled and has seven gates. It is less than a mile long and nearly all its roads are steep.

In England we cannot stand back and view our cities,

but from the plain the hill cities of Italy stand before us complete, like the bright pictures in missals, uncommercialised and ancient. They are also quiet, for their traffic is nearly non-existent, and only an occasional bell swinging visibly in a tower, a bullock-waggon, or the chatter of their inhabitants will disturb the silence.

Assisi is a mile and a half from its railway station, which in itself is a matter for thankfulness. On the extreme left, as one approaches it, is the Basilica of San Francesco, erected by Elias two years after Francis died. It is a gigantic building rising above a great retaining wall which is divided into arches perhaps seventy feet high. From below it looks like a bastion. It contains two churches of cathedral size, one over the other. A crypt is beneath them, and by their side is a widespread monastery. The town stretches to the right of the Basilica, up the hill in steep, twisted, narrow little streets, or corridors of stone, punctuated with many towers, for Assisi contains about thirty churches. Some of the streets are winding flights of stone stairs, and occasionally buildings are arched completely over them. Few of the roads have pavements, and many are only sufficiently wide to take a solitary waggon.

Whatever competition there is in Assisi, none is in evidence. There are practically no posters except small black-edged ones which announce a death in some family. Most of the shops have an entrance door in an otherwise blank wall. The name of the owner has usually been painted for so many years that it is well-nigh invisible. When the shop door is open the goods for sale are to be seen, when the door is closed the shop has entirely disappeared.

Motors are not unknown, but they are rare. The life and general appearance of this ancient town are therefore

pretty much the same as they were during the life of
Saint Francis. In spring the whole town is full of the
scent of flowers.

In almost the exact centre of Assisi is the market-
square with its municipal tower and an ancient Roman
temple of Minerva. But I think most of us on entering
the square would see first of all the great fountain, the
pigeons moving with consequence about it, and the
people filling their pitchers with its water.

Beyond the fountain, say, a hundred paces, and on the
south side of the market-place, there is a short road.
Through this one passes and finds oneself in a tiny square
behind the Communal Palace. This is Piazza Nuova,
containing a classical church surmounted by a dome,
built to commemorate the birthplace of Saint Francis.
The Friars will lead one to a stable behind the church.
"Here," they will say, "an angel led the Lady Pica
so that Francis should be born among cattle, and, being
laid in a manger, conform in all things to the life of
Jesus." Whatever one's views on that may be, and the
tradition does not go back to the early authorities, here,
within a few yards of the market-square, was Francis
born, and here he lived and spent his warm-hearted
boyhood. Recent discoveries completely confirm this
general position.

LXVIII

A burden of sin has been placed by the Church on the
youth of Saint Francis to emphasise his conversion.
But that he was always sensitive and generous is well
known. He was unusually generous, and whatever gaiety
he sought it must be remembered that he was a soldier
fighting Perugia at twenty. At twenty-one he was

imprisoned by the enemy and after his release was ill
until his conversion. At the worst his frivolity must
necessarily have been short-lived.

Just beyond the market-square is the gate called
Porta Nuova. The road which emerges from this overlooks a great portion of the plain lying some hundreds of
feet below. Here the youthful Francis used to stand
bewildered and sad, endeavouring to decide the path of
his future. Fourteen miles away on the hills across the
plain, its towers gleaming dimly, is the city of Perugia
where Francis had recently been imprisoned. "That
town," says the script, "hath a different memory in it from
Assisi; for many battles and wars were there in Perugia
in ancient times, and these have left a harsh memory in it
that hath none of the peace that is in Assisi."

And, indeed, notwithstanding its singular beauty and
its great art, there is in it an ancient and occult air of
pride, so that I was content when, after visiting it, to be
again in Assisi.

Still looking from Porta Nuova across the plain, there
is, to the right, Bastia, and just beyond the townlet of
San Giovanni which has a delightful mediæval bridge of
six arches spanning the Tiber. On this bridge was the
gay and knightly Francis taken prisoner. "Yea, I have
often looked at it," says the script, "and it bringeth
back the memory of my being imprisoned. I remember
it well. I remember what it was to be a bound and not
a free man. It was one of the threads that led me into
the way of better grace."

Perhaps the most prominent feature of the plain, say,
a mile and a half away, is the first and last church of
Saint Francis, surely the smallest headquarters that any
movement ever had which influenced incalculable
thousands of lives during hundreds of years. This is

Saint Mary of the Angels, or Portiuncula. Sixteen or seventeen seats fill it completely.

Two miles or so to the left of Portiuncula as we look down on the plain is Rivo-Torto. Outside the city wall, just beyond Porta Nuova and a little lower on the hillside, is the church and convent of Saint Damian. From this point of view it is buried from sight by olive trees, cypresses, and mulberry trees.

There is one more point visible from this gate. If we turn our glance from the valley and look up the great ravine of Mount Subasio, we shall see, grey-white against the woods, the little stone Hermitage of the Carceri into which Saint Francis and his Brethren often withdrew.

Francis had a wider life than Assisi could give him, but the places I have mentioned had a particular importance in the development of his soul.

LXIX

For a long time Francis gazed over the plain from Porta Nuova. He returned to the city and tried to catch once more the spirit of its gaiety, but again and again did he come back to this point where, from the shadow of the arch, he saw the plain lie before him with its forests, its wayside chapels, and its roads leading east and west. It lay before him like his own future. One senses that Francis perceived in himself power, as yet rather blind and unsure of its direction.

There came a day when he left the shadow of the arch and took a step forward. Presently he found himself within the dim and very little church of Saint Damian, dreaming at the foot of its great Byzantine crucifix.

" Yea," says the script at this point, " I will tell ye

of what happened. After I had left the fortress I was willing and glad to be free, but a strange thing had come to me, not a loathing of the old life I had led, but a sickening of it. And as I walked towards the lesser church it was in my mind that prison hath in it what death hath. That while I was within those walls something in me had died; and so I walked and was not mindful of anything but myself.

"And when I had come to the Cross I stood still thinking only of Francesco, and then a Voice spake to me. This Voice seemed to come from the Cross and yet was within me. And not in single words did I hear it, but as a sentence. And this it seemed to say : ' Ye are changed, ye are prepared, come unto Me.'

"It said : ' Come unto Me, this is My broken House. Ye shall build it again for the Glory of God. And this shall be a symbol to ye of what ye shall do later. So build My house, mend it ; ye must do this with thine own hands and hands that ye can find to help ye. Ye have lost and gained,' saith the Voice."

Those who care to enter Saint Damian will be shown where Francis rebuilt the walls and roof.

But the building is charged with history. In this small church did Francis undoubtedly begin his spiritual life. A few years later, Clare, a young daughter of a noble family of Assisi, came to Francis. She was professed in Saint Mary of the Angels and for her safety was taken to a convent in Bastia. Shortly after, Saint Damian was given to Francis, cells were built around it, and Clare took charge, and so was started the Second Order of Saint Francis, which really became her own order. The relations between Saint Mary of the Angels and Saint Damian form one of the greatest romances in spiritual history.

It is difficult to decide which building now most represents Saint Francis. His own church, Portiuncula, has had so much added to it and built around it, that a great deal of its ancient simplicity has gone. One has eventually, I think, to decide between Saint Damian and the Hermitage high up in the woods of Subasio. To my mind Saint Damian, as it is now, most completely represents all that Francis lived for. Its cloister is a garden. In May the acacias, which are all about Assisi, fill it with scent. The whole building, church, oratory, refectory, and dormitory, has that amazing smallness and simplicity which are yet so beautiful. Here are all the magic, the tendency to vision, the fire within the bush which hang like a nimbus around the personality of Saint Francis.

In some of its old rooms swallows have built their nests and fly fearlessly in and out of the open windows.

" This lesser church," said the script when I referred to Saint Damian, " is the home and house of Francesco, and so it is the house of his son. The great church is built for ceremonies that please the souls of men, but it is a temple and not a house and home for ye and me such as the lesser church. Ye are in thine home in that humble place. It was there that thy Father was first called to his Home."

LXX

On a door in the choir of Saint Clare there is a picture of Saint Francis, not as a saint, but as a youth with the sun in his hair, wearing a rose-coloured tunic and indeed dressed in all the gay raiment of the thirteenth century. He is said to have hidden in the deep embrasure of the door to escape the wrath of his father.

The little Friar who showed this to me explained that Saint Clare painted it with her own hand, and if she did not, she directed it to be done. I may be mistaken, but I certainly gathered the impression that Clare's view of the youth of Francis was not that held by many of his biographers. It is true that the Saint brought her to the spiritual life, but it is likely that her imagination had first been captured by tales of the lively, sensitive boy.

The Friar took a lighted candle from the altar itself so that I might see the painting more clearly. It was quite obvious that he cherished it.

I had never realised that Leo could draw until I saw among the relics preserved in the private oratory of Saint Clare a Breviary emblazoned by him.

Clare had her own garden, but it is a stone balcony rather than a garden in the ordinary meaning of the word. It has in it roses brought from Saint Mary of the Angels, passion flowers, and other growing things, and there are bright marigolds here and there. It overlooks a lower garden where grow vines and olives and lavender and rosemary. Both of these gardens overlook the whole plain of Spoleto which lies blue-green far below. It was to a cell in the lower garden that Francis, lamed and ill and almost blind, came after Alvernia. Here he wrote his Hymn to the Sun. Here, too, was he nursed by Clare herself.

The Friar who showed me these things, and with whom I have so often chatted about Saint Damian's, would choose very carefully two leaves from a rose-bush and one marigold, and quaintly and silently as I left would he hand these to me.

"No pride in him is there," said the script of him afterwards, "but abundant love that pleaseth Francesco, and he is well suited to the little place. Ye would find brotherhood in him. He is not as the priests are. He is content and feeleth his office natural and not a thing in which he taketh pride."

LXXI

When Francis prayed before the Cross of Saint Damian he had no other desire than to resolve the discords of his own soul. It was afterwards that he decided to preach, and then, while hearing Mass one morning, there came to him, with special meaning, the words : "Take nothing for your journey, neither staff nor scrip, neither bread nor money."

From that moment he delivered himself not merely of possessions but of desires.

"My Lord," he said to the Bishop of Assisi, "if we possessed property we should need arms to defend it." A sentence which has its own meaning to-day.

To quote again from Hester Dowden's script : "I will speak to thee of this, my brother," he says, "until ye have no possessions, and until ye know what it is to return to the state in which ye come and go from the world, ye have fears. When ye have naught and yet has God cared for and protected ye, then fear is gone. Then ye are fit to conquer men. In all this tribulation that is in the world must ye stand alone, happy with the little ye have and glad to show the others the joys of poverty as did I."

About the same time Ethel Green's hand wrote the same idea, more emphatically expressed : "For ye must give up all and pass alone and unknown to the place where I shall lead ye, where ye will find a need greater than ye can supply save through the hands of the Spirit. My son, trust thyself to my guidance and rest within my heart, for contentment doth not come from abundance of goods, but ariseth from a heart that rests upon the bounty of the Heavenly Father."

Such was the idea he formulated. Eventually it is the gospel of non-attachment. Perhaps Francis was one of the few men to preach such a gospel without hardness. But it is a singular fact that where a hundred hearts will respond to the call of comfort, a thousand will leap eagerly to life when Love urges them to hardship.

Little thought had Francis of forming an Order, but he had sounded a chord with the hand of a master. First came Bernard, then Pietro, then Silvester, then Giles. The joining of each is a Franciscan drama in itself. Already he had about him a nobleman who was happy to renounce his wealth, a peasant, and a priest who came in meanness but repented.

One wonders sometimes what unrecorded social difficulties were overcome by his genius.

With this strange and ever-growing Family went he about the little hill cities; gay with a boyish humour, having an almost divine irresponsibility and singing with happiness. The flowers seemed to grow at his feet and the birds gathered about his grey gown.

Who can resist the man who wants nothing for himself?

Such thoughts were probably in my mind as the hand of Hester Dowden raced over the paper, for the following was written unexpectedly:

"Now, my brother, have I somewhat to say to ye. This is as regardeth not only thine own life, but the companionship that thou hast with thy Father. I warn ye and admonish thee that not the grave and serious side of life must complete the man, but also the joyous and little side of the life of every day. With thy Father, after he was come into a full knowledge of the Greater Light, he sought all joy. Ye must remember that perfection doth not come in the destruction of joy, but in the selection of it. Ye can see that in the selection of joy is life made perfect, and the spirit hath in it growth in this enjoyment. All joy that cometh through the spirit and is seen with the eyes of the spirit goeth for perfection. But those joys that come through the flesh and go not to the perfecting but to the destruction of the flesh are evil."

And a little later : "Until ye understand the small things, ye can have no knowledge of that which is great. And until I was as poor as the birds themselves I had no understanding of the spirit and the value of the things of the spirit."

LXXII

Looking across the plain, as one stands by Saint Damian, two buildings are silhouetted against the misty blue of the hills beyond. The one to the right is Saint Mary of the Angels, which Saint Francis repaired after he had repaired Saint Damian. The one to the left with the small spire is Rivo-Torto.

There can be a silent loneliness about the roads of the plain. Low trees are grown in long regular rows and and over their lopped branches vines are trailed. These now and then give place to the grey-green lines of olives. Rain clouds rolled over the mountains as I walked eastwards. Saint Mary of the Angels lay two miles behind and Rivo-Torto was just ahead. The clouds rolled down the mountain-sides and down the ravines to the plain. Looking back I saw that they had covered all the hills around Mount Subasio, blotting them out completely save for one rent. In that gap, sunlit for a moment and completely encircled by a vast area of mist, hung the Little City, free and heavenly in mid-air.

Until he was about 27 the Group which had gathered around Saint Francis numbered only four or five men. Their only constructive ideas were that they must preach, pray, love all created things, and make no demands on anyone whatsoever. They had no Breviary, and for Office repeated the Paternoster. But they needed shelter, and there were sheds near the lepers' hospital at Rivo-Torto. My memory of Rivo-Torto is of an almost completely solitary church standing by the crooked stream from which the locality takes its name. This church was rebuilt after an earthquake in the middle of the nineteenth century. Within it are two rough stone huts preserved for the pilgrim to see. Whatever one's views may be of the huts, the general position is probably authentic. In these or in some similar shed did Francis and his Brethren sleep, and as they grew in number, each had his place and name marked out for him by chalk. Eventually the hut was given up with Franciscan courtesy to a peasant who brusquely demanded it as a stable for his ass.

I mentioned Rivo-Torto while with Mrs. Dowden and received these words in reply : " Yea, that place, too, hath a good memory for me, but not the memory that the Hermitage hath. In Rivo-Torto had I much struggle with myself, much to decide and arrange, and often I was perplexed. Ye need not doubt that this is the place, and a pity is it that a church should be built around the first home of the Brotherhood. Much could I tell ye of the life we had there and of the great strength that we had to find to approach the lepers. Ashamed of myself was I that I could not conquer the sickness that came on me when I approached these poor men, and that almost overcame me. Many times have I wept to think that these sick people had seen me shrink from them."

" I often recall the courage you had," I said, " when you turned back and kissed the first leper."

" That story," the script continued, "must ye take in this way. The kiss that ye speak of was not given in love to the leper, rather was it a test of the strength of Francesco. And although it had some value as courage in the sight of the angels, yet was it not precious as if it had been given in love that had forgotten what was horrible. I would not have ye think that Francesco hath in him what could be called saintliness. Courage hath he in him, he can force himself to do that which he hateth, but he had in him no love at first, but love for things that make the body full of enjoyment."

But the Family grew. When it numbered twelve Francis took them to Rome, and the Pope, blessing them, turned them officially into a preaching Order, and they called themselves the Brothers Minor. Francis had seen his appointed path, and sound vision always brings radiance. His renunciations had not been premature or forced; the flower in opening had simply discarded its sheath.

"In loss found I gain," is said in a script by Ethel Green referring to these times, "and in death was life revealed, so that I saw the glory hidden from the natural man, and truth was shown to me which the wise seek and find not. For as ye travel the path much must be left behind, and first do ye lay aside the material cares and desires of the body, then come ye to a place where the mind also must be purged of the weight it beareth. What hath hitherto helped now becomes a hindrance, for the strength of the whole being is needed to carry the white flame of Christ."

His rejection of all material desires had been complete, the white flame of Christ had become his light : " And," continues the script, " when the Greater Light cometh and lighteth up the spirit, that which went before is as if it were not."

LXXIII

The Order grew and needed larger shelter, and above all they desired a chapel of their own.

Late in the fourth century four pilgrims from the Holy Land visited the plain below Assisi, for here it was said angels used to gather to sing the praises of the Madonna. The land over which the angels sang was given to the pilgrims and was called " The Little Portion," or Portiuncula, and here they built a chapel and dedicated it to Saint Mary of the Angels. In the time of Francis it was the possession of the Benedictine monks of Subasio, but they, seeing the plight of the Brethren, gave it to Francis. It stood then in a wild forest. The trees, as Sabatier says, became its cloisters.

There is a curious resemblance here to the Glastonbury settlement of Joseph of Arimathea in that in both cases the twelve Brethren built themselves a circle of wattle huts about the shrine of Saint Mary and thus formed their convent.

Saint Mary of the Angels still stands. From one's window on waking in Assisi, or from various points in the little town where one sees the wide plain below, there will appear the far-off dome of Portiuncula. The dome is not of Saint Francis, it belongs to the great and rather cold-looking church built as a protection over it.

His most precious sanctuary stands under the dome at the crossing of the church, grey with years and very modest.

There are usually about seventeen praying-chairs in the little shrine and it is comfortably filled by them. The building—I speak from memory—is perhaps forty feet long and about sixteen to eighteen feet wide, and has a simple half-round stone vault for ceiling.

I doubt if it is possible to know of Saint Francis and to see this little House of Prayer without great emotion. It was, indeed, loved by him. It was here, curiously enough, that his mother, before his birth, came to pray that she might have a son. The very name " Little Portion," and the legend of the angels, charmed him. It became his home and the visible centre of the Order. Its modesty, its charm, its simple grace, all these were the very symbol of what he desired for his Brothers.

It was to Portiuncula then that Francis brought the Brethren ; here he lived while the direction of his life became clearer, and here his life came to fruition. As a girl Clare came to Portiuncula, Francis heard her vows and sheared the wealth of gold from her head.

In the first glory of his conversion Francis repaired this church as he had repaired Saint Damian. It is impossible to separate Saint Damian and Portiuncula ; though they are about two miles apart they are visible to each other. Saint Clare took charge of the one and Saint Francis of the other, and the relations between the two Houses were unique in religious history. It was Clare who removed the doubts that grew up in Francis regarding himself, and by clear insight rather than by sentiment gave him courage when he needed it. Their lives and their convents represent the two halves of one spiritual movement.

Sabatier speaks of the places connected with Saint

Francis as forming "a series of documents about his life quite as important as the written witnesses." Something of his soul, he says, may still be found in them. That is peculiarly true of Portiuncula, of Saint Damian, and of the Hermitage on Subasio. It is as though his fervour had made them radio-active, spiritually self-luminous.

It was from Portiuncula that Francis started on his great missionary enterprises to Spain, to Egypt, and to Palestine. These might be considered to be the climax of his work, but the climax of his own life was to come later. But recking nothing of "great" or "small" he went on his way and, being pure in heart, saw God. "In all that lives," says he in the script again, "God hath his image. Not in man alone, but in the smallest and the humblest is He manifested, the smallest flower or the smallest of the birds hath God in them." And again : "The love that grew in Francesco grew from companionship with the flowers and birds. These things that have love and beauty in them gave it richly to Francesco when he had a knowledge and understanding of them. The Brotherhood that was indeed a Brotherhood of love grew out of the flowers and birds."

LXXIV

That Saint Francis had a curious power over animals is probably too well known to need more than a passing reference. On his way to preach at Bevagna the birds flocked about him with such evident affection that he stopped and preached a childlike sermon to them, and blessed them. There are many similar references, and when he began the ascent of Alvernia it was the birds who welcomed him. But he returned thanks to their kind by buying and releasing doves that were being sold at Siena. There is, too, the episode of the little hare at Greccio which he released from a trap but which refused to leave him. The wolf of Gubbio I have already mentioned. This was destroying the children of the town, but Francis sought it in the wild places and gave it wise counsel. He then led it to the citizens and persuaded them to feed it. It became the friend of the whole town. Laurence Housman and, indeed, other writers before him have treated this story as though it were symbolical, the wolf being a human robber. This would seem to question the whole relationship of Francis to animals. In my view the general evidence is much too strong for his power to be doubted. An interesting fact pointed out by Mr. Goad of the British Institute in Florence is that recent excavations in Gubbio revealed the skeleton of a wolf which had apparently been given burial there within the old Franciscan church of San Francesco della Pace.

That he had that same natural understanding of men accounts for the extraordinary development of his Order. When he preached at Cannara, for instance, the whole population of the town wished to follow him, and he was obliged to initiate a Third Order which would permit of people living their normal lives, following their usual avocations rather than becoming wandering friars.

That Francis was no conventional ecclesiastic is, of course, obvious. Had he been less humble in his attitude to those he did not fully understand he might have been considered as being in revolt against ecclesiasticism.

One curious point which his mission shares with that

of Christ is that neither embodied any teaching in writing or put it into any form usually considered permanent, and yet probably no other men known to history have left so permanent and gracious an influence as Christ and Francis.

The particular result of the work of Francis was to extend the idea of God, to reveal Him in courtesy, in the great rhythms of music and in the beauty of words and in nature. He was particularly the artist's saint. He was the awakener of the Italian Renaissance. "No Francis, no Dante," has been said, and it might be added no Giotto or Fra Angelico. Indeed, it was as though he opened the hearts of three centuries to the view that rightly understood Love, Joy, Beauty, Religion, and Art were one, and that there were no barriers between any of the kingdoms of life. The flowers and the animals, whether bird or wolf, were his sisters and brothers. As Chesterton says : " All those things that nobody understood before Wordsworth were familiar to Saint Francis." Graciousness to all that lives, for which another name is love, such belonged, surely, to his own especial gospel.

LXXV

It was only the creative genius of Francis and his living affection for men that kept him from a life devoted wholly to prayer and contemplation. Such meditation he called " sharing the life of the angels." From time to time he withdrew from his fellows and sought it in the remoteness and silence of some mountain hermitage. There are many such hermitages associated with him in Umbria and Tuscany, but the one most closely linked

with all that he did around Assisi is the Hermitage of the
Carceri. A mountain-path connects it with Rivo-Torto
and with Portiuncula. It may also be approached
directly from Assisi by one of the easterly gates called
Porta Cappuccini. The walk is mountainous and takes
about an hour and a half.

On arriving, one passes under an arched building and
enters a courtyard. Everything about the Carceri is
miniature, extraordinarily picturesque, and childlike.
The chapel would surely hold no more than three people
kneeling. The age-blackened choir at the side is equally
small and equally lovable. This hermitage is in the
midst of a glen of ilex trees and ferns. Its north wall is
the rock face of the mountain. The south edge of the
courtyard has a low parapet whose far side plunges
precipitously into the ancient bed of a torrent below.
Very far below again, fifteen hundred feet or more, is the
plain of Spoleto veiled in blue haze with Portiuncula
showing as a dark speck.

Legends of the Carceri abound ; the well in the courtyard appeared mystically following the prayer of Saint
Francis. The torrent became dry when it was seen that
its quarrelling waters disturbed him. Birds and squirrels
gathered about him to hear his voice. Indeed they
gathered around the brown-habited Friar who led me
through the mossy ways to the natural caves.

" Is there any cave," I said to him, " in which Saint
Francis slept ? Or any connected with Leo ? "

There were indeed many caves, and one, according to
the Friar, was set apart for Francis and Leo. This I
entered ; it was a grotto rather like a small tunnel, a
little wider than a man, perhaps twenty feet in length,
and it ran through a spur of rock overgrown with
innumerable plants.

In London a few days later when with Mrs. Dowden, I said as she wrote : " I went up to the Carceri and saw the caves."

" Yea, Brother," came the reply, " ye need not tell me this, for there was I with ye, and ye wondered where was the spot in which I slept and ye slept also. Narrow was the bed, but enough, and I have seen many and wonderful visions with ye in that cave. Yea, Brother, ye did not think that in the narrow bed that often was damp, could I find comfort, but ye know that when the soul is uplifted, it heedeth not the body. The body that was accustomed to a soft bed could not bear the cold, it needeth cover. But it did not find the bed narrow, for when first I went there, I found that after I had lain down, there was a great Light in that place. Voices could I hear that spake to me, and I felt that soft cloths were put under and about me, and I had much love and care. And at times would the roof of the cave clear itself away, and I would see the sky and many presences in it. And ye have seen visions there, too, when ye were with me. The cave became a road that led me to another world. Good sleep I had there and it was a holy place to me."

Such words speak to my heart ; I can say nothing of them except that I feel them to be true.

Another script written by Ethel Green about the same time expresses an idea similar to the first part of this script : " As the spirit strengtheneth, the body becometh obedient unto it, and no longer doth it occupy a place of importance in the mind, therefore its sensations become dim and the centre of life and feeling is far removed and all thy being is wrapt in the golden vesture of the Lord."

LXXVI

It is possible for a few men to divest themselves of all possessions and to wander forth as preachers earning their sustenance by daily labour. The idea came to Francis as being the mode of life suited to his own nature. Others, seeing his spiritual freedom, hastened to join him. Such a company as shared the shelter of Rivo-Torto was still a practical concern. This small intimate group grew, however, in a few years to a band of several thousand. To many of these Francis was only a name, and some were mendicants rather than penitents. Such an Order having no organised system of life carries in itself the seeds of trouble if not of dissolution. Ten years after he had taken his little family from Rivo-Torto to Rome, Francis, travelling in Syria, received the first news of conflict among the Brethren.

It is not necessary here to discuss the whole trouble, but it may be said that the simple purity of life possible to one spiritual genius cannot become the order of life to thousands who have all manner of good intentions but no genius whatsoever.

Francis would have no compromise for himself; his spiritual riches, his discovery of God, his rapturous life of poverty were so real that possessions were an encumbrance, the most innocent desires, a prison. " Thou art Joy and Gladness, Thou art all riches in abundance," he sang later. His great passion was to bring the world to the place where he stood.

It was here that he met tragedy, for the world generally is not ready, is not nearly ready for the radiant and complete emancipation that Francis knew.

Ultimately a few shared his life; the others of his Order built themselves convents, gathered their stores of food and riches and learning, and became just another monastic order; good enough and sensible, but not that band of free and flaming Troubadours of God for which Francis had striven.

"Know ye," says a script of Ethel Green, "that thy Father passed through doubt and sorrow and saw the work of his hands fail him. Yet the Blessed One was ever near and the losses of earth were turned to triumph when He shared the pain. For what do ye live save to venture all and to find in Heavenly Love thy glory and thy crown."

When, desiring to keep vigil during the fast of Saint Michael, he set out with Masseo, Angelo, and Leo on the long walk to Alvernia, he went as one who knew that the work of his hands had failed him.

The shadows were crowding down upon him as he went out silent with the Brethren, for he knew within himself that he was about to meet darkness and storm and strange beauty. He was to be buffeted with temptation, to be consoled by music from Heaven. He was to oppose the dark forces of evil, to speak in the night with God, and to know the pain and everlasting gentleness of Christ.

LXXVII

From Assisi to the Mount of Alvernia is, by road, a little over ninety miles. Both the Tiber and the Arno rise near the mountain, and it is known that Francis followed the upper valley of the Tiber on his journey. The road one would use more naturally from Assisi to-day, however, passes the reedy shores of Lake Trasimeno with its solitary island still dreaming of the vigils of Saint Francis; by Perugia, by Cortona with its tomb of Elias and its

Hermitage of the Celle, almost as memorable as the Carceri, and through the busy streets of Arezzo. A rough mountain road fifteen miles long, often strewn with great boulders, leads from the final little town of Rassina to a high plateau about two hundred feet below the summit of Alvernia. I shall not speak here of the chapels, of the loggia with its frescoes, or of the beautiful mediæval monastery, for these are not of the day of Saint Francis, and belong to another kind of history. The far side of the plateau plunges down by precipice and windy scarp for three thousand feet to the valley below, which itself is a thousand feet above the sea. One stands here before a noble view of many peaks. I remember these as blue, seen through the vivid spring-green of the beeches, and touched with the gold of a strong sun. Alvernia is a mountain among mountains and remote from the traffic of men. It was here in this high place that Francis caused a cell of branches to be built for himself and, a little way off, leaving him hidden, were built cells for his Brethren.

It is often one's fortune to be disappointed with scenes having immortal associations, but as though the angels still guarded it and held it in affectionate thought, beauty has been heaped on Alvernia. Around and above the plateau to the summit are great beech woods and craggy ravines of strangely balanced rocks, mossy and set with ferns. There are dells and grottoes and torrents and ten thousand flowers. Above all, perhaps, there are great choirs of birds. This is indeed the mount of Francis.

Forty nights and days did Francis spend on Alvernia, and it is written that " during all that time of fast, a falcon that was building her nest hard by his cell woke him every night a little before Matins with her singing and the beating of her wings against the cell and went not away until he rose up to say Matins."

The story may be read in *The Little Flowers*. Leo was to attend him, but to keep apart, for Francis knew intuitively that some crisis, some culmination of pro-longed spiritual effort was at hand. A password was arranged whereby Leo could communicate with him. If Francis replied they were to say the Office together. There were times when there was no reply, but the anxious heart of Leo drew him towards his friend. It is to these stolen visits that we owe the record of this holy season.

There were many marvels, and in the silence of the night it is said that Francis was caused to see his own heart beside the diamond clearness of God. Again, there was music from a viol so profound "that his soul melted away for very sweetness," and he was lifted at another time bodily from the earth in ecstasy. Once there was a flame "exceeding beautiful and bright" from which a voice spoke and demanded three things : Obedience, Poverty, and Chastity. And we may be sure that Powers were present to search the heart of Francis and make vivid and real to him all that he was finally renouncing.

Again, there was a time in the early morning of the day of Holy Cross "when the whole Mount of Alvernia appeared as though it burned with bright shining flames that lit up all the mountains and valleys round as though it had been the sun upon the earth." And it was in the midst of this that there descended a Seraph and he was told "certain high and secret things, the which Saint Francis in his lifetime desired not to reveal to any man." And when the Seraph had departed he found in his hands and feet and side the five wounds of Christ's passion. And in his heart burned a new ardour and a new power, the argent flame of the Morning Star. For the Seraph had been his Lord. Heaven itself had come down to the Little Poor Man who had never asked anything for himself.

We shall never know the full tale of Alvernia, what fiery stars pierced the nights, what wisdom and clairvoyant beauty descended upon him as he prayed and fasted. There is a strangeness about the whole story, a supernatural air which the mountain even now reflects, an occult light which nevertheless is comprehensible to those of simple heart. We know that here in some way marvellous to us he met death yet remained in the world; and that here was he born into eternal life. Marvels emerge naturally around one so childlike in faith, and even as we feel within ourselves that he tamed the wolf of Gubbio, so we accept the heavenly music of Alvernia, the coming of the angels, and the vision of his Lord.

LXXVIII

One of the most impressive moments I had in Assisi occurred in the Sacristy of the Great Church. I had been speaking of Alvernia to the Guardian of the Monastery. He opened the door of a tall cabinet and placed in my hand the parchment not only written by Saint Francis and containing notes written by Leo mentioning the Vision and the Stigmata, but written on Alvernia itself during that amazing fast of Saint Michael.

It was, of course, the " Blessing " which Saint Francis gave to Leo. The Guardian explained that Leo had worn it, a point which interested me as confirming a note in the scripts of six months before.

As we might expect, the document had had a whimsical beginning.

Francis while praying for his " little family " was made
aware that Leo was troubled about his sins. " Wherefore
Saint Francis called him to him and made him bring ink-
pot and pen and paper and with his own hand wrote the
praises of Christ."

Before giving this to Leo he turned the parchment
over and wrote the passage from the Book of Numbers :
' The Lord bless thee, and keep thee : The Lord make
his face shine upon thee, and be gracious unto thee :
The Lord lift up his countenance upon thee, and give
thee peace.'

Under the writing he then drew a large headless cross,
or Tau. This he handed to the Brother begging him to
keep it diligently until his death.

But still pondering it and desiring to make the gift
even yet more affectionate, Francis took the parchment
again and wrote : " Brother Leo, the Lord bless
thee."

A moment ago I referred to a script which had mentioned this document. It was written in June, 1932, by
Hester Dowden and was as follows : " Yea, and I will
tell ye why this was done. The dear Brother was much
vexed in his spirit and I had not succeeded in driving out
from him a feeling for his sins. Thus did I say : Ye must
go back to simplicity, and as those that are simple do
hang charms around the neck, so wear ye this. And so
I wrote those words."

The parchment was referred to again in the script by
Geraldine Cummins written in November, 1936. It
occurred among the first words of the script when an
endeavour was being made to prove the identity of the
writer : " Brother," it said, " dost thou remember the

prayer ye wore around thy neck ?   Ye were always able
to face the day fearlessly when it hung about ye."

LXXIX

When Saint Francis left Alvernia he travelled to Assisi
by easy stages, for though he was possessed of a marvellous joy, he was a sick man.   He was also lame and
nearly blind.   He called at Portiuncula and stayed there
for some little time, but set out again, actually to go to
Rieti to consult a surgeon.   Although he was carried it was
thought wiser to take him no further than Clare's garden
at Saint Damian.   Here a hut of reeds was built for him
in which he lay while Clare nursed him.   It was in this
garden that he wrote his Hymn to the Sun.

Recovering somewhat he was taken to Rieti where the
surgeon, hoping to heal his sight, cauterised his face
between the eye and the ear with hot irons.   With many
halts for rest he was taken back to Assisi, not to Clare's
garden, but to the Episcopal Palace.   But death was
closing in upon him and he wished to be back at Saint
Mary of the Angels.

As one stands before this little church, to the right and
somewhat behind is a stone cell where a lamp perpetually
burns.   To this cell, after pausing on the journey to bless
Assisi, was he carried, and here he died.   With him were
the Brethren and the noble Roman Lady whom he called
" Brother " Giacoma, and to whom he had once given a
lamb.

Whether music like a fountain of gold lifted her voice
to him, whether he heard the ripple of harps, or the
heavenly sweet viol that sang to him on Alvernia we are
not told.   But a very simple and lovely thing did happen.

A great company of larks gathered together from all the quarters of Heaven and settled on the roof of his cell; and as he passed to where Love awaited him, they sang ecstatically.

LXXX

Comparisons have been made between the modesty of Saint Francis and the great size of the Basilica which Elias built to his memory. I confess to being untroubled in this respect. The Basilica appears to me to represent not so much Saint Francis as the tremendous affection in which the people held him. And whatever else it may be, it is a happy gathering-place for all sorts and conditions of men. In my visits to Assisi I always gravitated to this church, and when the weather was warm I would sit on the low wall in front of the Upper Church watching the people below. I mention this particularly as the matter was referred to in the scripts. But during my December visit the weather made it practically impossible. My feeling for the church had nothing to do with its architecture, for of this I am critical. . . . But it seemed to me to be a store-house of the world's joy in Saint Francis.

It is quite possible that sentiment at the time of the building of the church was mixed. Elias, for reasons which must have seemed very good to the older Brethren, was not liked. There is a legend that Leo smashed a bowl placed by Elias outside the growing building to receive gifts of money towards its completion. If this actually occurred it probably represented a passing irritation rather than a deep-seated opposition to the scheme. In any event Leo bequeathed to the Church what must have been his dearest possession, the parchment from Alvernia. Clare, too, when ill, was so anxious

on one occasion to attend worship there that tradition
says she was by spiritual means transferred bodily and
was seen at prayer before the altar.

In the crypt of the church are wonderful associations,
for here at the entrance is buried " Brother " Giacoma,
the lady who joined no order but who loved Francis and
all he did and for whom he sent when dying.

At the crossing of the crypt is left, projecting through
the floor, part of the living rock of the mountain. On this
rests the stone coffin of Saint Francis. An altar is in
front of it and a lamp burns above. At the four angles
of the crossing are the remains of four Brothers : Angelo,
Leo, Masseo, and Rufino.

The early December dusk grew to have a charm for
me when the bells in many towers droned and gossiped
together and I could cross the cloistered square and enter
the dark cave of the lower church for Benediction. The
Italian mind has its own lively attitude towards great
ritual which seems happy to me, and I ask nothing better
than to share its joy amid the frescoes of the Basilica.

LXXXI

One enters the church by what is, ecclesiastically, a
north porch. In an enormous and almost completely
dark vestibule sits a Brother at a table reading his prayers
by the light of one candle. As one walks, monstrous
shadows, reaching to the vaulting above, are cast over the
old walls. Quite unexpectedly to one's left, but far off,
appears the altar. There is a mystery about this altar,
for between the columns of the little arcade which forms
its base there is a pale light. If one could mount the
steps and look down through the arches one would see

the flame which burns over the body of Saint Francis, for the altar is immediately above it.

There are perhaps two hundred people standing about, a few sit on chairs of which there are only a score or so, for no great church in Italy has many seats.

The building is comparatively low with wide half-round vaulting. The altar stands not in the chancel, but at the crossing. About a hundred monks file in and sit on two sides of the altar with a choir of men and boys in the apse. The segments of the vaulting, bright with angels painted into loveliness by Giotto and dimmed by time into great loveliness, meet over the great candles of the altar.

There is an immensity of darkness out of which loom the heavenly meadows and the singing figures of the frescoes. Silhouetted against these are the worshippers divided into little dark groups. Rising above them are six triumphant candles, about twenty feet high and a line of four, only slightly lower. No other decoration, no fresco, no sculpture could take the place of these proud flames. With the smaller tapers there are altogether about eighty candles grouped together in this one place. There is no other light in the church. In the vast darkness they become a golden fire. The music and the incense stream about them, and the organ, fighting valiantly against the lusty plain-song of a hundred monks, has a grandeur all its own.

There would be moments when, in the fire over the altar, burned the transparent gleam of something other than candlelight. But the clang of the bell as the Father lifted the Host would change the dream. Nevertheless, I could never worship in that church without feeling the presence of a second congregation, ancient and hidden.

And even though Francis preferred the little things to

the big, he loved men and he loved beauty, and here, if you will, you can find the spirit of the Brethren and of him; for, as I said, this church in its vastness and mystery represents the affection of the world which still remembers him, and Francis is never far from the affectionate heart.

There is a script by Ethel Green which seems curiously to echo the comradeship and inner music of the lower church : " My son, when thine eyes are open, ye will be overwhelmed by the wonder of Creation and by the beauty of the spirit-world; for now are ye at the door and at any moment the portal may open for ye.

" I am with ye by day and by night, waking and sleeping, in sunshine and storm, when ye smile and when ye weep, in all thy actions, in all thy thoughts. I am the sun by day and thy moon by night. In the starshine and in the dew of morn shall ye see me; and as twilight falls shall ye hear my voice.

" I am with ye in music and in song; in all that ye accomplish, in thy dreams and in thy hopes. Thy soul is sacred unto me, for I bear it to the altar steps of God."

LXXXII

The final quotation may now be given from the script of Hester Dowden which followed so closely my movements during the December visit to Assisi of 1932. " Francesco is here," said the script, " to tell of what happened in the town in which I was born; for between ye and us was a fair veil that was thinner than it is in this country. When ye were there a change came upon ye. A place was made by which the spirit could enter in; I bade ye go to the Little Town for this purpose.

" In the Great Church when ye entered there were two that stood each at the side of the door, and on entering was there a change in ye. Ye must have felt that presences were all about ye, but most were they in the crypt.

" There was the Brotherhood assembled. I had called these from the four winds of Heaven. All but Leo, for Leo was there at the side of the veil that we could see through, though he could not see us. So, my dear son, ye took thy place among us, not for the first time. For before, when ye were at Assisi, were we there ; but not in such an order or bodyguard as this time. Ye were at home, my brother, and it seemed strange that ye should ever leave us again, and loath were we to let you go. For in the Church was a sweet harmony and companion-ship that gave ye peace of mind. Those that were in the flesh were not aware of us as ye were. These are good men and true, and faithful are they to the memory of me, but love can they not give me as ye give it. It comes to me as a sweet perfume from a meadow full of flowers.

" And now I must tell ye that in the lesser and much dearer church were ye with me alone. The Father shareth his own spirit with his son. For that ye were prepared at the ceremonial, which was a preparation for a greater blessing. Then when ye went to the Little Church the blessing poured itself in on ye. As the dove came down at the Baptism so did the spirit of thy Father enter into thee. No ceremony was there in the Little House, but there we sat together and in peace, and once came Clare to see her brother in the flesh.

" It was sad for me that ye could sit for such a short time before the door of the Great Church. There I had hoped to give ye a manifestation of my presence. But in the Little Church had we deep and sweet communion."

LXXXIII

The purpose of this book is now nearly fulfilled, yet a great number of scripts have been excluded. I recognise acutely how great this omission is, but many things which may quite simply be stated in intimate conversation may not be written in a book. The personal element in each has a different value.

It has been noted elsewhere that neither Christ nor Francis made any effort to put their wisdom into writing or into any recognisably permanent form. Now if their essential contribution towards the upliftment of mankind was embodied in the words they spoke, this is at least remarkable. Is there possibly some mystical element involved in both cases which we by no means understand ? For their work did live. Was it that actual life-essence was passed by them to those who could receive it ? When Francis died there was for some centuries a new creative activity, for the world burgeoned into the beauty of the Renaissance.

I am suggesting that Christ and Francis belonged to the same Order, an Order which can, by the gift of Spirit, not by teaching merely, make the world fruitful. This essence, when reference has been made to Christ, has been called " the Blood," to make clear how much it is of the essential self of the giver. Granting the incomparable grandeur of Christ, I suggest that Francis was not an earthling, leaping in imitation of the eagle's flight ; he was in fact a young eagle. He was of the same kind. He had wings.

That all men will eventually serve their brethren by giving of themselves seems certain. Whether all will serve in this particular way is not clear. There must in any case be a diversity of effort.

A script written by Ethel Green early in 1934 speaks of the " Sons of Light " or the " Sons of the Kingdom " and, though the point is not stated, it seems obvious that it is to this Order that Francis belongs :

" . . . they carry the undying flame, the beacon which showeth succeeding generations the road to immortality.

" For to the Sons of the Kingdom is this Light given, and it is that which revealeth the new way of life to the maturing soul of man ; for each age receiveth its own illumination, and man requireth continually new teaching and a fuller insight into the laws that govern the universe and into the Being in whom he dwelleth.

" To the Sons of the Most High is entrusted the task of apportioning the revelation to the growth and needs of the children of earth. These High Ones dwell nigh to the Centre of Life, but their children are found at all stages of progression, and their call is always the same. The cry for Light from birth to birth breaketh from their lips ; and never can they cease their search until the glory of the Life Triumphant sweepeth them into the ocean of Light that beateth upon the shining throne of God.

" At all times these Sons of Light are blessed, and though their sufferings are greater than those of their companions, even in their darkness are they aware of an ecstasy and a thrill ; a movement of life beyond the narrow bounds of their being, a chord in their hearts which is in harmony with Nature's choir.

" They are the ladder on which the angels descend ; they are, as it were, the nerve centres of the body of humanity, receiving impressions both from without and within and transmitting their inspirations for their fellows who can perceive but through them."

LXXXIV

That Francis has some especial relation to our own period seems certain. That he is present in men's minds is manifested in many ways. During the last fifty years there has been an increasing literature about him, and to him a great number of churches have been dedicated. There has been a tendency to clothe Christ in strange ecclesiasticisms and theologies until He is well-nigh hidden. Many have turned to Francis recognising that they may get another and a clearer view of the real Christ, as He was and is, through him. My own view is that Francis in this time of terrible trouble has drawn nearer to the earth to make his own great gift towards simplifying the confusion in which we find ourselves.

I quote from one of the last scripts written by Ethel Green.

"From the Spring of Life do I speak unto ye and declare His will, even He the Master whom the Golden Worlds have crowned Victor and Deliverer. Through me, the least of His servants, doth He speak to this generation and offereth Himself again in the soul made in His image, and subject to Him in all things. Therefore do I return to Earth bearing with me my Lord, and seeking mansions of flesh where We may dwell and spread abroad the glory of Our Being, the Light of Perfection shining through the spirit that is Francis, the Little Brother of all Mankind.

"This is my day given unto me of the Father, wherein I suffer once again with the wounded and the sad, and bring the joy of an unclouded morn to eyes that gaze across the sombre wastes, dim with sorrow and unshed tears.

"I lift once more the burden of the weak, and lay myself down in the dark haunts of sin that I may rest awhile with these dwellers of the depths, and waken in them the instinct to cast off the swathings of the animal soul and rise to the purer air.

" With all men will I partake, and the beggar's crust shall be as sweet as the delicacies of the rich ; for to the souls of men do I call and to them I show the beauty and the gaiety of the untrammelled life, the immeasurable Love which guardeth each one, the infinite value of the human soul, and all the wealth of unimagined splendour which is its heritage.

" I shall preach the Gospel of release, the escape from the prison house, the opening of the eyes of the blind, the cleansing of the heart and the gift of the spirit of eternal youth to the glory of my Lord before whose beauty I am speechless with the burden of my joy."

LXXXV

In chapter forty-eight of *The Little Flowers of Saint Francis* will be found these words :

" Brother Jaques of La Massa, unto whom God opened the door of His secrets and gave perfect knowledge and understanding of the Holy Scriptures and of things to come . . . beheld in a dream a tree fair to see and very great, whose root was of gold and its fruits were men, and they were all of them Brothers Minor. . . .

" There arose a storm of wind and shook the tree so violently that the brothers fell down to the ground. . . . And so long did the storm beat against the tree that it fell, and the wind carried it away. Then, when the storm ceased, straightway from the golden root of this tree there sprang up another tree that was all of gold. Of this tree, and how it spread out its branches and fixed deep its root, and of its beauty and fragrance and virtue it were better to keep silence than to speak thereon at this present."

That was written seven hundred years ago. This, surely, is the secret time of which it were then better not to speak ? Is it not even just now that Francis awaits the blossoming of his fragrant tree ?

From the scripts I take this very simple call : " In all humility must ye live, giving of thyself to all who are in need, for greatly have ye been blessed and greatly must ye give."

" In the time that is coming, need will there be for stout hearts and strong. For tribulation will be upon the earth, sounds of weeping and of woe, and darkness shall be upon the people.

" So I call to ye to take up thy Cross, and look not behind ye, for the future is all glorious and full of wonder."

His call is now, as always, to the sad and whimsical and to those weary of pretence and self-importance, and who hesitate in judgment, to those who no longer cherish contempt, to the picturesque dwellers in the wilderness, to the love-children, to those of the singing heart, the troubadours, the brave artists, the mummers and bedraggled poets, to those who have lost their treasure but remain content, to those who have denied their Lord, not once but thrice ; to these he calls. For though they may have great weaknesses yet, like she of the ointment, many have true knowledge of the elements of Love and have not subordinated life to comfort and safety. Their freedom has already begun and in due time will be completed in their Father. Their laughter, which so gaily hid tragedy, will spring anew to hide the fierce tears of their joy in homecoming.

POSTSCRIPT

*" Though I stand within the shadow, yet
shall ye feel my presence ; and through
thine own will shall I lead ye."*

Francesco of the Scripts.

IN a letter to Ethel Green, I mentioned that the word
" Ye " is used in many of the communications in a
manner which does not conform to the standards set by,
say, the English translations of the Bible. Her reply
was to send me quotations from Milton, Shakespeare,
and many of the lesser Elizabethan poets. These
make quite clear that its use, as in these writings, was a
commonplace of the sixteenth- and seventeenth-century
literature.

That, however, though justifying the general form of
speech, does not explain why the Francesco of the scripts
should use a seventeenth-century manner. The particular
use of the word " Ye " and of other peculiarities of
speech may, of course, be in actual fact, mannerisms of the
communicator. It is possible to conceive, if one accepts
the theory of reincarnation, of the previous personalities of the communicator surrounding his essential self
like the facets of a diamond, and that restrictions are
imposed by the limitations of the particular facet through
which he is manifesting. But even if that is so we have
still, in the present case, to explain the use of English,
for it was unknown to the communicator.

In a script to Ethel Green, received in 1938 through

her own hand occur these words : " We have given ye the key with which ye may enter that enchanted world and bring back . . . pregnant thoughts which, nurtured in the mind, will clothe themselves with words. . . ."

When Francis knelt at the Cross in the Church of Saint Damian, a voice, as from Christ, came to him. The words through Hester Dowden which refer to this incident are : " This voice seemed to come from the Cross and yet was within me. And not in single words did I hear it, but as a sentence."

The clue seems to be here. Both of these quotations suggest that communications from those " in the spirit " do not always come in individual words.

We can, if we will, be conscious of our own thoughts, like electrical charges, before they have taken form in speech. I am inclined to think that the transference of similar charges of unspoken thought is responsible for most of these writings, and that the medium, recognising the atmosphere of an earlier century, subconsciously supplies an expression of a bygone time which is not necessarily correct historically.

It seems probable, too, that thoughts originating in levels higher than our own, are sent down the planes through relays, " stepped down " as it were, probably one relay for each plane intervening between the place of origin and ourselves. If this is so, inconsistencies of expression are understandable.

Whatever the explanation, I have thought it proper to present the scripts as they came, and only occasionally have I made minor alterations, such as the omission of a redundant or too personal word.

In the main text of the book I have also, for obvious reasons, altered some of the names of places and of living persons. Otherwise the book is a simple and true statement.

It occurs to me that there may be those who would like to see excerpts from some of the scripts which have not already been used. These are given below. It has been necessary at times to make excisions; indeed the most beautiful of the writings will not be found in this book, but those which are set down are without the interruption of comment.

Practically all the scripts received through Hester Dowden have been included in the text of the book. Many trance sittings are, for one reason or another, unsuitable for publication in full, for though often evidential, they are mostly too intimate. I have decided, therefore, to form a postscript composed entirely of writings received through the hand of Ethel Green. These, at my request, she has selected herself.

March 14th, 1933.

I am with ye in thy downsitting and thine uprising, and in all that thou dost.

I rest on thy spirit like the dew of evening and pervade ye as the perfume dwells within the rose.

My light is around ye, and my love guardeth the threshold of thy heart.

March 21st, 1933.

Give heed unto my words, for I have much to say unto ye this night.

My power is upon ye and I will lift ye up to the heights where dwell those who have been filled with the Spirit, who have come through the flood and through the fire, and in whom strength hath been made perfect in weakness, though of themselves were they naught. For the strength is not in *ye*, nor should ye look within thine own being for that which shall exalt ye, or bring ye to thy heart's desire. The spirit taketh the weak, the feeble, and such as have no trust in themselves, and of these doth it forge weapons for the honour of the Master. Yet the instrument in itself can do nothing but wait upon the pleasure of its Lord. So, my son, look not to thyself, but know that thou wilt be used according to the will of Beings too far removed from earth for ye to comprehend, yet who can enter into thy person and make of thee what they desire.

It is thine to give thyself and to offer thy will so that ye may be a living sacrifice ready to obey the behest of thy Spiritual Lords, the Princes of the Kingdom of the Soul. For a mighty company is with ye gathered from the four winds of Heaven ; and ye, and those with ye who know of the wonders of the spirit, and have faith in the hand that leadeth them, will be used to show that the Unseen ruleth in all things, and that the visible world is but a shadow and a symbol of the eternal. My son, put thy trust in the Life which is in all created things and of which thou art a fragment, and wonder not if marvels be done through ye, or if ye be called to wander on a strange path, for those to whom the spirit cometh must give up all and follow wheresoe'er the vision leadeth them.

Thy power dwelleth in thy faith, and as ye believe so shall it be unto ye. Therefore, my beloved son, look not on thy weakness, for thy Father knoweth thy nature and he will not expose ye to the cruel thorns nor to the jagged rocks until he hath covered ye with his vestments and shod thy feet with strength.

My son, my blessing is upon ye and ye shall share my vision and my joy : and thy Father will bear thy sorrows and comfort ye in thy distresses.

May 17th, 1933.

Many years ye have sought and have sighed in vain ; darkness enveloped ye and thy soul wandered in the desert places, but the time of trial hath passed, and from henceforth thy spirit shall walk in the light of an ever-increasing revelation.

Seek not after knowledge, but trust to thine inner guide, for all things will now be taught ye from within ; for thy Father who dwelleth with ye will himself give ye the key to many mysteries; and wisdom shall dawn within thy mind as naturally as a flower openeth to the sun.

Before ye face the world I desire that ye be fully developed, so that we can guard ye in all danger and know that thy being will respond at all times to the forces we shall bring to bear. We shall use spiritual weapons against a fleshly foe, and need to have complete control of our medium of expression.

Man can strive with man, yet the world doth not advance ; but now will the Lords of the Spirit World enter the arena clothed in the robes of their children ; and naught can hinder their victory, nor the triumph of our Lord the Christ, Who will be ever in the midst of the battle. . . .

Yet when the Powers of Darkness seem to reign supreme they shall be overthrown, and the time of their triumph shall be the hour of their defeat. For the Eternal Father useth Evil as a means to Good ; and from the ruins of one stage of life doth He bring forth a higher state where man shall grow nearer to His Image.

My son, ye shall bear thy part in this world renewal, and will build to the honour of thy Father, not with stone nor brick, but with human hearts and lives, a Temple in which the Master will dwell.

May 29th, 1933.

Obey me and abide in humility, and I will bring ye to the inner knowledge from whence ye shall gaze on the world of sense, and perceive the limitations from which thy brethren suffer, and thy heart shall be pitiful so that ye shall desire to give thyself wholly for their salvation and enlightenment.

For only as ye become perfected can ye guide others, and only as ye learn can ye teach, and only as ye become rich in the heavenly gifts can ye succour the poor and oppressed.

Therefore, my son, chasten thyself and look ever to the inner man gazing upon Him Who hath passed through all which thou canst suffer and Who walketh with ye in ageless Perfection and Beauty, revealing to ye the Life to which each of His children is called by the Eternal Father.

I would speak to ye once again of my joy in ye and the future which is radiant before ye.

For the day dawneth and the night hath passed, and thy soul hath entered a higher state where ye become aware of thy divine origin and the continuity of thine existence.

June 3rd, 1933.

This is the day of opportunity, for the soul of the world is awakening from her long sleep, and wisdom shall no longer be the privilege of the few, but the mysteries of the Divine Life shall be revealed to the simple and childlike, to such as have love within their hearts and purity in their souls. The Master hath prepared these to receive His teaching when it shall be given to the world, for during His days on earth He spake in parables and even those nearest unto Him understood Him not; but now will He speak plainly, lifting the Veil and showing the Eternal Purpose, and the Glory of the Son sacrificed from the beginning of Time in the Creation of the Father. No words can declare His love or paint His Beauty, but we His servants reflect His Light and rejoice in His Presence, bearing on our breasts the burning jewels of our devotion for Him, the Wonder of the Universe, God in Man, Infinite and Sublime.

June 8th, 1933.

My children shall preach naught which they do not practise, for with them first must come the life by which they shall show their unity with the Spirit of the Divine in man and Nature; and having accepted the bond which linketh each to all, they shall receive power from the Highest, and no state of existence shall be too lowly for their comprehension and their love.

For how can ye understand that which is above if ye understand not that which is beneath, the root from which ye have grown; for all the forces of earth and nature have nurtured ye, and thy spirit hath climbed through many forms and by many stages.

June 20th, 1933.

Strong must be the links between earth and Heaven before we pour forth upon ye and thy companions the anointing oil by which ye shall be consecrated to your appointed tasks. And brightly your faith must burn before we can pierce the mists and clothe ye in our Light ; for as ye reach upwards our hands are stretched to thine, and we hold ye in an enduring clasp which will carry ye through the murk and the morass to the mountain heights and the glorious vision of the children of the Sun, resplendent in their angelic sphere.

My son, thine outward life will be humble and filled with material difficulties, yet within shall be the vision and the song, the life that bloometh in the Eternal Spring, and the joy that filled the Stars of the Morning as they sang together.

The power that cometh from on High shall lift ye up, for naught can withstand the cleansing tide which floweth from the Heart of the Infinite, and to this River of Life have I brought ye, my beloved son, that ye may be purified and possess in its fullness the Divinity which indwelleth the soul of man, and mouldeth it to the Image from which it sprang.

Rest in peace, for round ye is the Light of my protection, and the promise of the coming day ; for all that I would, that shall ye do.

August 21*st*, 1933.

In the coming days my spirit will be strong within ye, for much that was thine hath now perished, and the Father hath a more spacious temple within thy soul wherein he can effect a greater control over thy being. For there is in ye less of the earthly kingdom, and thy feet are upon the shining path which leadeth unto the Perfect Day.

Ye have been tried and buffeted by the strange force which men call Fate, but which we call the steps of

Destiny; for there is no blind bludgeoning, but life is a sequence of events each of which hath its purpose and effect; and infinite care is given to each unit of the Universal Spirit. Yet in no way can we control the will, but each is free to refuse the call of the Great Father. Yet to all the offspring of the Eternal Spirit cometh the hour when the voice is heard and the Divine element is raised from its deathlike slumber.

Then cometh the hunger of the soul for the Heavenly Manna and the long search until the creature resteth in the Creator, and having fulfilled the purpose of its being, entereth into the Harmony of the Celestial Choir where life is music and where thought is praise.

September 21*st*, 1933.

My strength is sufficient for ye, and in me shall ye rest, for my life is filled with the overflowing Love that createth the smallest creatures and maketh each perfect and complete.

Outward knowledge shall not advance ye, for all true growth is from within, and is a refining of the soul, an inbreathing from an higher world; so that the perceptions become more acute, and a wider range of vision is offered to the sight.

Then do ye see even as also ye are seen, and personal pride fadeth away, for it can find no place; and all that ye have been is dead and void, for the seed of the Eternal springeth up, rising on wings from that dark shell, a thing of Beauty and of Light, called from the dust and destined to the Stars.

We, the Servants of the All Glorious, seek for such as crave the Heavenly Vision, and having found them, burst their bonds asunder, and release them from the trammels of the earthen sheath. Sharp are the pangs of the new birth, and feeble the spiritual child emerging into an unknown country. Yet to these, the little children of the Kingdom, cometh the Blessed One, and gathereth them in His Arms, giving them strength that they may follow wheresoever He may lead them.

October 1st, 1933.

Listen to my words, for I speak to thine inward ear, and for the instruction of thy spiritual being. Ye are now developed to a point where I can show ye what shall transpire not long hence; for now that ye have pierced the veil and have been restored to thy place among thy Brethren, greater power will be thine, and the fabric of thy physical body will change, and will become a garment in harmony with the soul which is thine essential self. So that ye shall no longer be trammelled by inherited instincts and habits which are part of the burden which ye chose to endure when seeking to serve thy Father on the plane of Earth. Thy roots were buried deep, my son, beneath the soil, and many years have passed before thy spirit saw the Light of the Day it had known, or felt the joy of the Eternal Dawn.

Yet now are ye come to conscious union with thy circle of power, and with him who sent ye forth on thy perilous journey. Ye have drifted to the shore of thy sea of Forgetfulness, and the waves will break over ye no more, for now the Angels take charge of ye, and all that hath been shall again be thine.

October 4th, 1933.

I return to ye at this hour of peril when the future of humanity trembleth in the balance, and the Holy Ones are gathered as birds before a storm.

I am come to prepare ye, and the time is not yet; more I cannot say, for the Future may not be revealed, but to my son I show the portents and the signs, and bid him gird on his armour, and discipline his soul, and cast from him the gawds of earth. For to the Pure in Heart will the Light come when darkness enshroudeth the outer world.

My son, we pass by strange ways and under the Shadow of the Cross, and mortal strength will avail ye nothing, nor can ye choose thy path; for One walketh with ye, even He who bore extremity of Woe, and with Him shall ye experience the height and depth of man's capacity for joy and sorrow; and He will teach ye all things, and bring all things to thy remembrance, for ye have offered thyself, and await thy Call.

October 22nd, 1933.

Ye have received my words and have obeyed my behests, therefore can I reveal to ye yet more of the weaving of the Pattern prepared by the Mighty Ones.

Much hath been accomplished since first I wrote through the hand of this child, for ye have received thy Baptism and have passed through the Valley of Humiliation thereby ascending to a closer kinship with thy Father and receiving the recognition of thine ageless companions.

Ye have journeyed through the mist and through the cloud, and thine eye hath seen visions of the Glory that lieth beyond the span of Time. Ye have supped of sorrow and yet have found Life within the Cup, and the wings of thy soul have grown strong and have borne ye far from the dwellings of earth. Therefore, my son, take courage, for not in vain is this time of preparation.

Ye are being fashioned by the artificers of Heaven and must be perfected against the day of Trial when the blessed One leadeth forth His Chosen, and Divine Love will vanquish the Shades of Death.

October 30th, 1933.

No longer may ye be stirred by the emotions of sense, nor let the lamp of thy spirit be dimmed by earth-born clouds, but ye shall be as one apart, lifted above the restless waves of turbulent thought and unceasing desire, to a still Air where broodeth the peace of Infinite Conception and Accord.

For as ye find refuge in the Mind of the All Pervading Spirit, so do ye realise the true abode of the awakened soul and the grandeur of thine inheritance.

In the silence shall ye find Wisdom, and by waiting upon the Source will thy portion be received.

November 20th, 1933.

I would speak to ye this night of the perils of the way, for ye shall meet many obstacles on thine upward path such as beset all those who seek to climb the heights. For ye pass into a strange country and breathe a purer air, and where ye were weak ye shall become strong, and that which hath been powerful in ye shall dwindle away ; for all things have become new, and many factors in thy life must be readjusted.

Ye must be in harmony with the Father who dwelleth in ye ; and where ye fail, there will be discord and distress, and thy mind will be rent and divided against itself. Look neither to the right hand nor to the left, but be single in purpose, accounting for each day to thy Master, knowing that the time of thy preparation draweth to a close and that still ye have much to learn.

For round the Earth the clouds are gathering, and the air is angry with fierce hatred and dissensions, and none can say where the thunder will break forth.

But the dove of Peace shall descend and find its home in the Living Temple that I build, and my sons and my daughters shall minister therein and naught shall make them afraid, for in the Power of the Presence shall they pass unscathed where terror reigns.

November 22nd, 1933.

Do not hesitate to place all thy gifts at the feet of the Christ, for no sacrifice that ye can make will be too great for that which we desire to attain. Let no darkness within thy soul hide from thee the glory of thy Destiny nor let the frailty of the flesh rob ye of thy Robe and Crown.

We who protect ye and give ye of our Power, who have revealed to ye thy condition and rank among thy peers, we also have passed by this path, have worn the thorns upon our brow and have grown faint beneath the burden the Master had laid upon us. Yet the brief moment of struggle passeth, the life given is returned an hundred-fold. For he who giveth to the Infinite Father receiveth of His Glory and shineth for ever among the Sons of God.

December 14th, 1933.

The time hath come when the mysteries of the age shall be revealed to all who desire light upon their path that they may approach the Centre of all Power and Life.

For a new spirit is within the world and man throweth
off his leading strings and will no longer follow blindly
the blind leaders. He will accept instruction only from
those who can perceive the Invisible and hear the
Unspoken Word ; who are filled with the Spirit and who
speak with Inner Knowledge, and have escaped from the
bondage of creeds and the inherited beliefs of past
generations. For the soul of man requireth freedom for
the growth of the new age and strength to carry the
burden of greater responsibilities. Therefore upon many
will be poured forth the gifts of the Spirit that Light may
penetrate the darkness, and humanity be reborn nearer
to the Divine Image.

This is a Day of Days when many forces meet and much
is shattered in the impact ; yet in the Infinite Mind is the
Supreme Thought, the Creative Urge towards perfection,
and we who dwell in the Eternal Harmony are at one with
these vast waves of Power, and all our being is given to
this invincible direction of the thought forms of God.

For His children work each in their degree and the
Power is transformed by the creative activity of His
ministers. For there is no break in the chain between the
least and the greatest. The Creative Power floweth
through all, and each is a partaker in the Divine Plan
and giveth that which he hath to the Universal Heritage.

December 21*st*, 1933.

I would bring ye cheer, for ye are weary and heavy-
laden, and the cares of the world weigh upon thine
heart.

Yet shall ye withdraw thyself to thy Mount of Joy
where the Father dwelleth with ye and the Blessed Ones
are gathered from their far Hills ; and there will thy

youth be renewed and the days of earth life be seen as a dream which remaineth but for a while; a shadow through which ye pass to a more enduring glory.

Rest in my assurance that all is well, that naught can destroy the power of the link which we have forged, nor separate thy soul from him who hath begotten ye and who travelleth with ye through the dark valley. For even as ye encounter temptation, and are visited with sore distress when the Spirits of Darkness would enshroud ye in their sable wings, ye shall find that there is within ye an abiding Hope and a fervent Purpose by which ye shall withstand the power of the enemy, so that even the gates of Hell shall not prevail against thee. For thine hand touched the Robe of Light that He wore Who passed before ye, and He will draw ye through the fire and through the flood till ye rest at His feet, thy long quest ended.

January 15*th*, 1934.

As ye see with the eyes of the spirit the aspect of creation changeth, and ye look from within, from the Eternal Unity to the diversity of the outward manifestation, and thy mind becometh a part of all that hath proceeded from the Infinite Mind. No longer are ye aware of thyself as a separate unit, but ye realise that when ye are one with Christ, then doth the Great Father give to ye the freedom of His Home, and thy finite existence is left behind; for it cannot hold the glory of the Universal Life which hath been begotten in thy soul.

Thus are the bonds of the lower self broken, and the mortal hath put on immortality.

My son, no words can paint the wonder of the Greater Life to which each of earth's children is called; but it can come only by the rending of the outer vestment, the stripping off of the personal desire, the purification of the fleshly garment. And as ye don the robe of sonship, all that hath developed ye as a separate entity will be required no longer, and will be as valueless as the husk of the ripened grain, or the nest when the brood hath flown.

All the experiences of life have their purpose and are stages which must be passed through, but when the experience is completed, he is at fault who lingereth and faileth to pass on to further tests and greater endeavours.

For the children of the Highest are His treasure and His joy; and marvellous is the design by which they come forth from the Great Deep of Infinite Beginning and grow in beauty till their light filleth the Heavens and the Father Himself seeth that they are fair.

Praise be to His Name Who hath made the lowliest of His creatures ministers of His Grace, lifting them from glory to glory till they are restored to the Fount of Life from whence they came, and to the Order of the Godhead which is theirs.

Thy father, Francesco, who leadeth ye this step upon the Way.

January 22nd, 1934.

Ye have wandered far from thy home, but thy father hath called unto ye and ye have heard his voice; and the lamp of his love guideth ye through the veils of darkness and of gloom that clothe the outer world where ye dwell.

And as he leadeth ye step by step, ye shall learn the lesson that each day giveth ye; and ye shall find that time will unfold the blossom of thy life, and bring forth the fragrance of thwarted effort and uncomprehended love, so that all the mute endeavour of what ye

thought the wasted years will be garnered as graciously
as the ripened fruit when summer wanes.

For no thought and no desire can be destroyed once
the mind hath given it birth; it is the seed that ye sow
from day to day and from year to year; and when ye
come to the season of fulfilment of the harvest of earthly
life, then is revealed to ye the hidden growth which
thy mind hath made fertile, and which is the garland that
ye bring to the Beloved from out the realms of Unreality.

For the fruits of evil thought are made manifest to ye
during the days of thy struggle, and ye must meet and
fight the phantoms which thy mind hath created in hours
of weakness or fleshly pride before ye can set thy feet
upon the starlit path. But the delicate wraiths of beauty
and of purity which have issued forth when thy mind
soared toward Eternal Truth, await the time of the final
dissolution of the outward frame; and gather round the
soul, adorning the ascension, and heralding the approach
to the Kingdom of the Unbegotten.

January 25th, 1934.

There is a time to gather, and a time to disburse thy
wealth; and ye have come to the day when ye shall add
no more to thy golden store; but ye shall learn of the
simple things of life, and find thy God in the curved petal
of a rose, or in the smile in the eyes of a child.

For wisdom is like the symbol of the Circle, and endeth
where it began; yet carrying with it the fullness of
maturity and the faith that cometh from the inward
vision of the soul.

Thy circle neareth completion, therefore I say unto
ye, learn the lessons of the heart; and so shall ye find the
key to perfection, and understand the Love which linketh

the celestial harmonies and draweth the stars in their courses through the pathless Deep.

February 5th, 1934.

When ye have received thine accolade and are true knight of thy King, when thine honours have been won and the fierce battle lieth behind ye, then are ye called to be as a mirror for those who follow after ye and to reflect for them the beauty of thy Lord, that through ye their eyes may be opened to the glory of the soul that weareth the robe of flesh as sweetly as the petals clothe the rose.

For the Divine must be manifested through the outer garment, that men may see the grace of Him who shineth in all the works of God, but most excellently in that masterpiece of Nature earth's fairest child, the soul that biddeth its farewell to the splendour of the sea and sky and bathed in the radiance of a brighter sun, passeth beyond the verge to paths untrodden and to worlds unknown.

February 19th, 1934.

I will speak of the vigil of the Grail and of the vision that cometh with the flush of dawn. For to those elected to bear the Life Blood of the Christ is shown the vision of the Cup from which the world's Redeemer drank His bitter draught of earthly woe.

But now the Cup is no longer a symbol of sorrow, but is embellished with the Light of victory and carrieth within it the Heart's-ease of Heavenly Love ; so that those who gaze thereon are for evermore the servants of their fellows, and are banded together by a mystic link by which they are both warrior and priest.

He Who entered the fleshly veil and bore within Himself the sufferings of Mankind, hath overcome the separation of the Human Soul from the Divine and bridged the gulf which lay between two stages in the development of Man; so that in Him the child of earth can ascend, while still in the body, to the kingdom of the Christ.

Therefore is the vision of the Cup given to those who make new paths from earth to Heaven, to those who plough the barren lands and make the desert bloom; for they, too, are of the nature of the Christ and adventure their souls in strange places, seeking ever their Father's face.

At all times will He be their guide; and the Brotherhood of the Holy Grail will minister unto them, and they shall drink deep of the Cup of Life; for the sorrow of earth shall be changed to joy, even as He turned the water into wine.

March 3rd, 1934.

At this time shall the tangled threads of former lives be unravelled and all shall be woven into the eternal Pattern; so that whereas ye were many ye shall become one, formed in all completeness and shining with the ray whereto ye were born before the earth was shaped or the moon languished in the summer sky.

For life hath no end and no beginning, but the manifestations of life succeed one another as the shadows of the clouds flee across the mountain-side. A time cometh when the shadows pass, and the reality which they image forth doth emerge, clothed with the beauty of the traversed worlds, each of which giveth of its richest gems to that pilgrim soul as it passeth on its illimitable journey to the Golden Heart of Life.

February 4th, 1935.   *L'envoi*.

For as I gathered round me in my days on earth the sweet singers of the woods and the little flowers that perfumed the mountain-side, since all things of innocency and beauty were my delight, even so now do I draw into my magic circle the souls that are like unto the simple creatures that gave me joy and friendship ; those that know not the sweetness of their secret song, nor the beauty of their soul that the Heavens have nurtured and adorned.

For in my Household the poet and the child are found ; those who play upon the chords of Life and upon the rushes by the river's bank. The simple and the subtle shall both know me as Master, and the richness and vitality of my life shall flow through them. For I am of the Sons of the Morning, of the bow that shineth after rain, of the Golden Cross that throweth its light athwart the night of Time.